Sammy Davis, Jr.

A PERSONAL JOURNEY
WITH MY FATHER

TRACEY DAVIS

AND NINA BUNCHE PIERCE

RUNNING PRESS

PHILADELPHIA · LONDON

Books published by Running Press are available at special discounts for bulk purchases in the United States by corporations, institutions, and other organizations. For more information, please contact the Special Markets Department at the Perseus Books Group, 2300 Chestnut Street, Suite 200, Philadelphia, PA 19103, or call (800) 810-4145, ext. 5000, or e-mail special.markets@perseusbooks.com.

ISBN 978-0-7624-5017-6
Library of Congress Control Number: 2013953904

E-book ISBN 978-0-7624-5064-0

9   8   7   6   5   4   3   2   1
Digit on the right indicates the number of this printing

Designed by Joshua McDonnell
Edited by Cindy De La Hoz
Typography: Berkely, Lato, and Riesling

Running Press Book Publishers
2300 Chestnut Street
Philadelphia, PA 19103-4371

Visit us on the web!
www.runningpress.com
www.ratpacpress.com

Dedication

To Sam, Rae (Montana), Greer, and Chase.

And to Pop.

Contents

My parents and newborn me, July 1961

Introduction

My father, Sammy Davis, Jr., was an entertainment legend who created his own rules to overcome the prevailing racism of his day. Over the course of six decades, from the 1930s to the 1990s, he was at turns a comedian, actor, dancer, singer, and member of the infamous Rat Pack in Las Vegas, with Frank Sinatra, Dean Martin, Peter Lawford, and Joey Bishop. But he was also a father—my beloved "Pop."

I told his story once before, in my first book, which was published in 1996. It was a more standard "reading book" with a small photo insert. This time, in addition to recounting stories of his life and career and my personal memories of Pop—including a great many that didn't make it into the first book—I included many more personal photographs to lend a sense of immediacy and a more intimate touch when reading about my father's extraordinary life.

Even more important to me than sharing photos, though, I wanted to revisit my father's life with the grace of time having passed and emotions calmed down, to put everything in perspective. I now have four children and many years of experience as a parent to give me new insights on my own relationship with my father. In my family, we still talk about Dad in the present. My youngest ones, Greer and Chase, have learned about him through me. We'll be driving across country listening to his music, and I'll hear, "Mommy, tell me about Grandpa Sammy." Through these conversations and stories, I started to reflect on conversations between my father and I. I realized that I now felt so much more positive about our time and the difficulty of the situation, and I realized how vital those conversations were in my ability to move forward without him.

I also decided to tell his stories in a different way—to the best of my ability, the way he gave them to me. After getting throat cancer, my father became particularly nostalgic about the past. This book has an unusual setup in that it focuses on a rare, intimate time between my father and I. In the last four months of his life, from February to May 16, 1990, my father deeply reflected on his life. He was dying and I was pregnant with his grandson, Sam Michael Garner. Pop was determined to live long enough to see the birth of his grandson, despite the doctor's prognosis that he would not.

Deep down we both knew that the horrible ugliness of his disease meant there was no turning back, no getting better, which created a freedom for me and Pop to speak freely. For once, no subject was off the table: rude jokes, past slights, misunderstandings, laughter, and love—above all love. During this time my father shared his most personal and precious life stories with me. Depending on the story his memories were told with intense passion, joy, comedy, or sorrow, but always with deep feeling and so vividly that they have remained with me ever since, unforgettable. I may not be the raconteur my father was, but I recount them for family, friends, and his fans as best I can. This book is primarily based on our father-daughter conversations in the hospital and his home in Beverly Hills. It's not possible to recall our conversations word for word, but, thankfully, there are a wealth of letters, articles, research facilities, and friends and family I could consult with when necessary to verify facts and jog my memory.

I cherished the opportunity to recapture my father's past again while putting together this book. I hope that you too enjoy this personal journey with my father, Sammy Davis, Jr..

Chapter 1:

Growth

A portrait of my father in 1963

When my father, "The Entertainer," a black, Puerto Rican, one-eyed Jew, got throat cancer and died, well, I just fought with God. After everything he'd been through, was this some kind of sick prank? He was suffering from a cancer that made its presence known every day by a tumor that protruded on his neck from the source of his illness—his throat, once the source, at least to my mind, of the most outstanding voice in show business.

The irony of it all was an epic tragedy to me. He was so frail he took on the semblance of a caricature of his former self—one of the greatest entertainers of all time, who also happened to be my beloved father. I stood by helplessly, pregnant with my first son, overwhelmed by the reality that my father was going to suffer and die without ever meeting his grandchild. Pop stayed strong, but it often seemed more than I could bear. The struggle between God and I raged on for months, but I still prayed and prayed that Pop would hang on long enough.

I remember vividly one night waking up from my sleep, in utter panic, having an out-of-body experience. Things and places, past and present circled around me in the dark. As I tried to climb out of this terrifying abyss of uncertainty, it was right there before me: the future. In a flash, I was with my husband, putting my newborn baby into my father's arms. Was this a premonition? Was God working up some kind of miracle? I didn't know, but I decided to give God a break. From that night on maturity set in. It was God who gave Pop all his talent. Perhaps the true test of faith is how you face death. In light of the gifts God gave my father, I had no right to regret his impending death.

Dad sure got a lot into sixty-five years as a performer. He was on the vaudeville stage by the age of three, packed in over forty albums, seven Broadway shows, twenty-three movies, television-show-host spots, and zillions of nightclub and concert appearances. He was a five-foot-six-inch, one-hundred-twenty-pound legend. As my father would say, "God gave me the talent, all I had to do was not screw it up."

What a journey it was of pure talent and sheer determination to triumph as the world's greatest entertainer amidst all the racial adversity of his day. My father was a bona fide star, used his talent as a weapon to fight racial indignities, created his own rules, and planned to leave the world just as he wanted—to quote him, "while I'm still interesting." Pop was dying and I didn't want to miss a minute of it, no matter how bittersweet. If my father was going to do the death march, I was going to march right by his side.

When Pop got sick, I was pregnant with his grandchild. Starting a mere few months from delivery of my child, on April 20, 1990, cancer ravaging my father's throat, we spoke more than we had in my entire life. Conversations took on new meaning. We were laser-focused on Pop's life, knowing each time I saw him could be the last time we talked. Later, he would hold his trachea tube just to speak. But we talked and talked, treasuring each word with

In 1961 the world was curious as to what the daughter of Sammy Davis, Jr. and his "Swedish goddess" wife would look like. I'm about five years old here, just coming into my own "look." As my father neared the end of his life I was soon to give birth to my own interracial child—one I hoped my father would live long enough to meet.

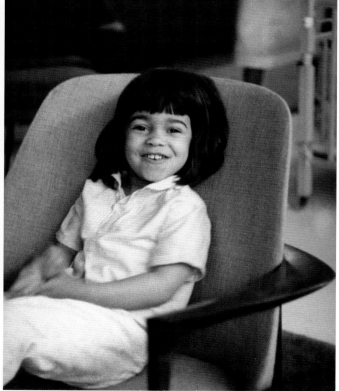

impending urgency, in a manner infinitely more rapid and spontaneous than ever before.

We were together all day, every day—a far cry from the days when Pop didn't even know my phone number. Typically, an assistant would call and send for me. It was liberating just to saunter through the front door of his Beverly Hills home without being sent for. From death would grow life, so I started my journey back in time with my father.

"Hey, Trace Face, you get uglier every time I see you," his eyes sparkled with joy as I entered.

Pop's 1151 Summit Drive estate held fond memories of years of Hollywood entertaining, his most proud moment being my interracial wedding to Guy Garner inside his 12,600-square-foot home. Pop's most sacred sanctuary was his 2.5 acres of lavish emerald gardens with pungent eucalyptus trees and a sparkling pool. It was a tranquil oasis where he could drink in the air and reflect. It is where my father would spend the last days of his life.

His gourmet kitchen in the guest house was his pride and joy, back in the day. Pop loved to cook. Lessie Lee Jackson, who started as our nanny but ended up a family member, was Dad's prep cook. Lessie Lee was the estate matriarch. Her most infamous line to my father's third wife was, "I was here before you, and I'll be here when you leave." Lessie Lee in her slippers and old Southern house coat, would often saunter across the lawn to the guest house kitchen to deliver the ingredients for my father's favorite chicken cacciatore.

On this day, Pop held court behind the brownish downstairs bar off the living room, pulling the sides of his V-neck cashmere sweater down over his designer jeans. From time to time, his nurse, doctor, or private armed guard would pass by, but we never paid them much mind. I sat on a bar stool, praying my pregnancy weight wouldn't topple me over. I was confident we would have some privacy that morning, no celebrity visits from Uncle Frank (Sinatra), Liza (Minnelli), or Bill (Cosby).

Pop caught me staring at his raw pink blasted neck where the second round of chemotherapy radiated his dark skin pigment right off. Even his Aramis cologne couldn't diffuse a smell of sickness in the air. But to mask my sorrow, I allowed the cologne to assume its olfactory guise. I surrendered all my sensibilities to its soothing artificial semblance of reality.

"I'm doing all right, Trace, just tired." Dad winked. "Want a Strawberry Crush?"

"Coke, please, and maybe something to eat," I replied. Pop hollered into the kitchen, "Lessie Lee, whip up some smothered pork chops with rice, I think we got a craving here!"

"So, Trace Face, I'm thinking about pulling out the pool table in the bar upstairs and making a proper nursery for when you and the baby come over," my father announced.

"Are you going to pull out the bar, too?"

"Let's not get ridiculous!" Pop smiled.

Dad poses with his Rolls Royce outside Piccadilly Station in Manchester, 1961.

"How about the racks of guns on the wall from Clint Eastwood, Elvis, and all of them?" I asked.

"Never mind. We'll put the nursery in the guest house!" Dad smirked.

I could tell an ominous shadow followed a deep reflection that enveloped my father's eyes today. "Bet you wish you could turn back the clock, huh, Popsicle?" I often called my father Popsicle.

"Perhaps, but childhood, I don't know. I never was a kid," my father said.

"You made damn sure we got the best childhood, Pop. But I guess you missed out, huh?"

"I never realized there was a childhood to miss!" Pop said. "Show business was a particular world unto itself. When I was three years old, doing two or three vaudeville shows a day, I couldn't just go out back and play with the kids. I didn't know how. I didn't even learn to read or write until I was seventeen and in the army. I never had any formal education like you, Trace Face, never spent a day in school. So guess what?"

"What, Pop?"

"Baby, I'm going back to school!" Dad howled.

"You mean for your GED?" I knew Pop had no idea what a GED was.

"Nope, I'm going back to the first grade!" he said. "Dip into that well! Learn my lines! Sing some ABC's to that kid bursting out of your belly!" Pop knew his ABC's, but I wondered if he could sing the

I love this picture of Pop, smiling and happy.

song that accompanied it. My father spent the first ten years of his life like a mimic when it came to anything outside of entertainment.

"Just teach your grandchild how to play 'Fool the School.' You mastered that role." He gave me one of his warm, twinkling, father-daughter smiles.

"Fool the School" was a game Pop played back in the early 1930s in his Harlem home on 140th Street and Eighth Avenue with his grandma, who raised him. He called her Mama. She was a heavy-set woman with joy in her heart, a happy face, and the "black-attude" of "You come around here again, I'll beat your butt with this broom!"

From about the age of six, my father would rehearse his rat-tat-tap dancing in the living room for that evening's vaudeville show. Mama would guard the window, watching for truant officers who could potentially mess up Pop's rise to fame by throwing him into school. When Mama spotted one of the truant officers, they would both freeze in place. "Don't move. Don't breathe," Mama would whisper, as she listened to the slow, steady pace of heavy boots entering the building, each footfall climbing creaking the wooden stairs.

Dad never went to school a day in his life, never knew the first thing about literature, but the way Pop told the story, it felt like Edgar Allan Poe's black raven flew smack into the middle of Harlem! Suddenly there came a tapping, a white man gently rapping, rapping at their rickety ghetto door. Deep into that darkness, peering long, Pop stood there at six years old—wondering, fearing, doubting, and

LEFT: My dad and his own father, the man who started him in show business.

ABOVE: A congratulatory kiss from his mother, Elvera, after the opening of *Golden Boy* on Broadway, 1964. Although raised by his grandmother, my father's own mother remained on the outskirts of his life.

dreaming dreams of stardom no "colored" mortal ever dared to dream before.

Dad learned quickly that a white man in uniform rat-tat-tapping on their ghetto door, somewhat louder than before, only meant trouble. Startled at the stillness broken by reply so aptly spoken, his soulful, willful, don't-mess-with-me Mama would whisper her own words of wisdom to Pop, "We can wait long as he can knock, child!"

My father was born on December 8, 1925, in Harlem, as an only child to vaudevillians, Sammy Davis Sr., an African American and Elvera Sanchez, a Puerto Rican. My father always joked that Elvera's father was so prejudiced he didn't even like black shoes. The two separated in 1928. Elvera continued her career as a chorus girl. My grandfather raised Pop with his own mother, my great-grandmother, "Mama." Pop always felt abandoned by his mother, never cared for her much, but he fronted in public and paid her rent for life. As the story goes, Elvera visited Pop on the vaudeville circuit once when he was just a kid. His father introduced them, "This here is your mother, Elvera." My father's response was, "What? I have a new mother every night."

Dad's father promptly took his son on the road as part of the Mastin Troupe lead by Will Mastin. Will was not a blood uncle, but Pop always called him affectionately, "Uncle Will." My father began his rise to stardom playing vaudeville at the ripe age of three

years old. In 1928, he was already a little firecracker, sitting on a singer's lap onstage, imitating her facial movements with hearty laughs from the audience.

The Will Mastin Troupe had become the Will Mastin Trio: "Uncle Will" Mastin, Sammy Davis Sr., and a rising spark plug, Sammy Davis, Jr. Pop adored his father, the limelight, and wanted to be onstage more than anything in the world. My father saw a world where people would applaud you, give you credence, plausibility, a safe haven. The stage was a place where if you had talent, you could grab on to it and earn instant respect. In the early years Dad told me he often said, "What have I got? No looks, no money, no education, just talent."

I motioned Pop to sit down on his Gucci half-moon couch with me. Lessie Lee had placed our smothered pork chops and some beverages on the coffee table. Our soul food feast sat on the glass coffee table in the good company of Judy Garland's ruby slippers from *The Wizard of Oz*, sealed in a special case from Liza Minnelli. Liza was a longtime close friend of my father's, and they entertained together for many years. On the table was also my father's Kennedy Center Honor, letters from Jack Benny, and a bunch of belt buckles from old western films.

"Silent Sam the Dancing Midget is how they billed me, Trace Face," said Pop, "I was the freak of the show back in the day!"

The Geary Society in the 1930s had a law that

no child under sixteen could sing or dance onstage. Pop explained, "I would sit in the wings and watch the stage. I wanted to be in that gang but I was only four or five years old. I was in my element because I knew no other element. They had to bill me as a forty-four-year-old midget to work because I wanted to work. My father put me in black face, a little redundant, but they thought that was enough of a disguise."

Pop's eyes lit up, "Oh Lord, then it all came to a screeching halt at the Liberty Theatre down on Forty-Second Street! Here we are doing our act, making an impression, audience is loving it, then *boom!* Two beastly women and three white cops climb onstage. Guess they figured out I wasn't a midget! I hear my father yell, 'Run boy!' as the cops throw your grandfather to the ground and handcuff him. So I slipped through the officers, the midget

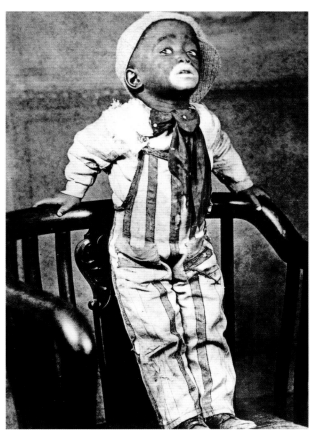

Black performers often appeared in blackface in the early twentieth century. This is one of dad's very first professional photos.

My father on stage in the early 1930s

that I was, and man, did I run!"

"Where did you run to, Pop?" I asked.

"Home to Mama! Where else? Hey, that was the way it was in show biz at the time. If you had to run, you had to run. Heck, there were adult performers running. Colored folk running was nothing to be embarrassed about. Just had to run sometimes, sign of the times." Dad smirked.

"What happened to Grandpa?"

"He was thrown in jail. Released with a date for a court appearance. Uncle Will got away somehow. Funny, even thirty years later, when I bought your grandpa that fine house in Beverly Hills next to his doctor's house, he still slept with a shotgun under his bed!" Pop laughed.

"I used to say to my father: 'Dad, who's coming over here to getcha? Your doctor? You gonna shoot him?'"

"And what did Grandpa say?" I asked.

"He would say: 'Son, you know nothin' about no safety, no how. You? You're gonna talk smack to me! You? Who sits with his back to the door *still*! Who's coming to get *you*, son?'" Pop laughed as he reminisced.

"What happened after Grandpa was thrown in jail over the dancing midget fiasco?" I asked.

"My father was to appear in court. Mama said: 'Ain't no one walking into that courtroom but me!' Mama stormed into that Harlem court on fire. Told the judge that my own mother, Elvera Sanchez, was chorus girlin' somewhere, no tellin' where she was. Mama said the only person fit to take care of little

ole Sammy was Mama herself! The judge had work documents from the house Mama cleaned with little white kids she raised, so he gave Mama full custody of me." Dad smiled.

"Mama must have loved having that power," I said.

"Oh, Trace Face, that day Mama came marching through our Harlem door on 140th Street and Eighth Ave like she was queen of the castle. Mama boasted to everybody, 'The judge said his own mother and father ain't capable of raising him, so he gave Sammy to me. Legal!'" Pop roared, slapping his knee.

"Bet Grandpa and Uncle Will respected Mama after all that!" I said.

"Utmost respect and a few little white lies to get us back into show business. Uncle Will made up some story about a big gig he lined up in Boston for us, paying money. Mama believed him and so did I," my father explained.

"Mama started asking me questions like, 'While you on the road, you ever been hungry, Sammy?' I told her the truth, 'No, Mama—Daddy and Massey been hungry, but never me,'" Pop said. He often called Uncle Will "Massey" back in the day.

"My father started packing bags and grabbed me to go. I said, 'Where we goin', Daddy?' He said, 'We're going back into show business, son!' And off we went."

My father's oeuvre of work as an entertainer was vast. But back in the 1930s and early '40s, Boston was no show business treat for Pop. The Will Mastin

The Mastin Trio in the late '40s: Sammy Davis Sr., my father, and Will Mastin.

LEFT: Uncle Dean, Pop, and Uncle Frank at their best.   **ABOVE:** My father in the "ring-a-ding" '60s.

Trio was homeless, sleeping on benches in train stations. Uncle Will would go up to the ticket counter every couple of hours to ask a bogus question, so they wouldn't be thrown in jail for loitering.

When the train station closed, the Trio moved to a nearby open bus station to catch some shut-eye on their benches. When it came time to eat, there was only enough money at the restaurants to order Pop a meal, so his dad and Uncle Will would leave with empty stomachs. On a lucky night, his father might put together enough money for a beer, anything to help ease the hunger pains.

"Ah, Trace Face, in those days, we were on the road, homeless and hungry, sleeping in terminals, hopping trains without no tickets. We paid our dues. Nothing like the scrumptious, delectable Sands Hotel '60s days in Vegas," Dad explained.

Six years after my father died, in 1996, the Sands Hotel was imploded to make way for the Venetian Resort Hotel Casino in Las Vegas. In an off-camera conversation, the Emmy-winning filmmakers of *Biography: The Rat Pack*, Luke Sacher and Carole Langer spoke with Vegas singer and dancer Claude Trenier, who said, "It's not like it used to be. I liked the old Vegas. I'm sorry they tore down the Rat Pack room, and the Sands, and the Dunes. . . . These were landmarks! And what kills me, it seemed like the new breed wanted to tear out anything that reminded them of the old Vegas. They wouldn't have the new Vegas if it wasn't for the old Vegas."

Back in its prime, Pop says, "The Sands was our 'Rat Pack' oasis, our home away from home. I hung out with Uncle Frank, Uncle Dean, Peter Lawford, Joey Bishop, and celebrities galore in a 3,000-square-foot plush suite. We ordered everything on the room service menu—spread out buffet style. Huge bowls of cigarettes with every brand in it—my Pall Malls or Camels unfiltered—whatever I needed, wanted, at my fingertips. When I was drinking, always had a Coke with bourbon on fresh ice handed to me by hotel staff standing by—or Strawberry Crush when I was on the straight and narrow. Rat Pack lifestyle. We owned Vegas, baby. We even had a private celebrity pool, not on the ground floor, mind you."

"Pop, you always liked everything first class. Even now, I wonder, why you pay for all this stuff?"

"Because I can, Trace Face, because I can."

In the 1930s and early 1940s the rise of motion pictures began stealing the light from vaudeville stars. My father, who claimed he was just turning five years old at the time of filming (the press mistake him to have been seven), made his big screen debut in "Rufus Jones for President," a musical short with Ethel Waters. Pop performed a little tap number, singing around a stand-up microphone, dressed in his Sunday best with a top hat and all. A bona fide five-year-old professional, he never missed a beat or a step. Pop always joked, "The film stunted my growth. I could fit in the same darn suit today!"

But Pop continued to travel throughout the

country as his father and Uncle Will trained Pop on tap dancing, singing, and how to engage the audience with a confident patter and a wide smile. My father told me the same story he once told talk-show host Richard Bey, "In those days in show business, speaking medically, the job was not to be a specialist, but a general practitioner—you had to do a little bit of everything, know how to say a line, sing a song, tap a dance, do a joke. It was part and parcel to our business."

Gradually my father became the trio's star, leading the act to larger and larger clubs. Uncle Will decided their pay would be split three ways. Years later, after Pop became a solo artist, he still split his pay three ways, paying Uncle Will and his father until the day they died. Pop was kindhearted, lavish, and generous to a fault. When my father was invited to private dinner parties he wouldn't just show up with three dozen roses, he would arrive with a gift from Tiffany's—that was Sammy Davis, Jr. style.

"I created my own rules, Trace Face. I danced, sung, joked, or impersonated my way through the color barrier. Like the time my father and Uncle Will told me I couldn't do an impression of James Cagney or any white artists. I couldn't see any sense to it and did it anyway. I did a Cagney walk to center stage, spread my legs apart in a classic Cagney stance and said, 'All right . . . you dirty rats!' There was a startled pause and then a roaring applause. Backstage, my own father apologized for being wrong, laughed, and hugged me. See, Trace, in

those days we had TOBA—that was an abbreviation for 'Tough On Black Artists,' and the 'A' . . . didn't always stand for 'Artist.'"

"I get it," I said.

"I don't know who made up the rules for 'colored' performers. But if you were colored you would never address the audience when you walked onstage. There was this invisible wall colored entertainers were not allowed to cross. When we worked downtown at the Paramount, the Roxy, Loew's State, the Capitol Theatre, the Strand, the 'colored acts' would come on the stage talking to each other like, 'Why ya yesterday say ta me . . .' This really got on my nerves. So, I went to the opposite extreme. I would walk onstage sounding like Laurence Olivier—'Good evening, ladies and gentlemen . . .' It was a personal challenge, too. I wanted to see how well I could speak with no formal education."

"But Grandpa and Uncle Will taught you everything else about the stage, how to tap, sing, capture an audience?" I asked.

"Pretty much, Trace Face—until the night I got to watch the best in the business. It was in the early 1940s at the Plymouth Theatre in Boston. We did our opening act, stood in the wings. The great Bill 'Bojangles' Robinson took the stage. His dancing was different than I had ever seen. He didn't do the routine flat-footed buck and wing. He skated on the balls of his feet. He had this shuffle-tap style that flew him backward faster than most could tap forward. My jaw just dropped open," he explained.

"Is that why singing 'Mr. Bojangles' was always

Dad performed "Mr. Bojangles" with more feeling than he did any of his other songs.

the signature segment of your shows, Pop?"

"Oh, it was deeper than that, Trace! After the show, we went back to Bill Robinson's dressing room. He had a valet helping him put on this silky monogrammed robe. Beautiful! I counted twenty-five pairs of the finest shoes laid out on the floor. Right then and there, I knew when I became a star, I would not just have one pair of Sunday best shoes. I would have a collection of designer shoes. Jerry Lewis and I used to talk about how when we became stars we would buy not one, but five pairs of shoes at the same time. We would do the same with suits, hats, bow ties. Tailors were sweet candy to us."

"You do have quite the wardrobe, Dad."

"Anyway, after I counted twenty-five pairs of Mr. Bojangles' finest shoes, he says to me: 'Lemme see you dance, kid.' My knees buckled, but I gained my composure and did a little tap number. That was the beginning of my tutorials with the best in the business, I was a young star in training." Pop smiled.

"Inspired by the best," I added.

"Bill Robinson was the cream of the crop—old school. Do you remember my sixtieth anniversary tribute, the one you couldn't attend a couple of months ago because you got in that horrible car crash?"

"Yeah, almost lost the baby, Pop," I said.

"If you had lost my grandchild, you would have lost me."

"I know, Pop . . . we're okay. The crash was my first childbirth lesson: I learned to breathe, count, and swear all at the same time! So tell me about the tribute."

"Well, at the sixtieth anniversary they did a montage of footage with voice-overs of me talking about 'Mr. Bojangles.'"

Pop continued, "Fact was, I could not do a show without including 'Mr. Bojangles.' Every finale, I performed that number. It was very special to me, hit close to home. I almost feel like it was written for me, but it was not. Nor was it written about Bill 'Bojangles' Robinson, as some people say."

"Who wrote it?" I asked.

"Jerry Jeff Walker of the Nitty Gritty Dirt Band for his 1968 album," Pop explained. "Jerry composed it about a white homeless vagrant he met in jail who called himself Mr. Bojangles. This white guy was down and out, drunk, talking about how his dog up and died after fifteen years traveling around together, making a buck off the remains of his talents wherever he could. So the inmates tried to cheer him up, asked him to dance across the jail cell. So I did my own heartfelt version of it. You remember my version, Trace Face?"

"Of course, Pop! I only watched you perform it a zillion times! You always whistled the melody opening that number." I remembered.

"Start out soft, make the audience strain to hear you, that's how you captivate them." Dad said.

"That song always makes me want to cry."

"Cry?"

"After your finale, fans would swarm me, 'Oh, you're Sammy Davis, Jr.'s daughter, you're so beautiful, blah, blah, blah . . .' it was just overwhelming."

"You're too sensitive, Trace Face!"

I'll never forget how Dad got me to sing that song with him on the spot that day—impromptu duet. Our indelible performance was a precious rhapsody that I would tell my children about in years to come.

Pop went on to explain, "I did 'Bojangles' the first time live with Tom Jones, in 1970, on his television show. In that skit, Tom sang the song by himself, while I silently played the part of Mr. Bojangles, dancing and doing routines in sync with the lyrics."

Pop started to relate the song to himself—a speech I had heard him announce in public before. "'Bojangles' was special because I hated the song. Well, I should say, I had a love-hate relationship with the song. I was afraid to do it because that was always my fear—that I'd end up like Mr. Bojangles

. . . drunk, alone, dancing in a jail cell."

"Surprise, surprise! You didn't end up drunk dancing in a jail cell!" I told Pop.

"But I still had the fear. I told the press, my fans, when I would do that number some nights, I would get so hung up on it. One night in Vegas, I said, 'Oh my God! That's me! I'm projecting! That's how I'll be when I'm seventy years old. I'll be working little joints, talking about what I used to be—and that'll be the end of it.' That man, that culmination of different black performers, minstrels that I'd known—performers who got hooked on junk, who got wiped out by alcohol, got wiped out by the changing of times—I'd seen them disappear, great dancers. But, Trace Face, I wouldn't end a show without 'Mr. Bojangles.' It was deep in my heart and soul, a spiritual journey through life."

"No one performed it better than you, Pop," I said.

"Damn straight." He cajoled and howled, hoping that his own laughter would distract us from the onslaught of his medical condition. I saw the exhaustion in my father's eyes, fatigue was setting in. It was time to rest and refresh.

"Hey, Pop, let me grab you a Strawberry Crush to perk you up," I said.

I headed over to the downstairs bar. I grabbed my father a Strawberry Crush and myself another Coke. I couldn't have been gone more than five minutes. By the time I returned to sit on the couch, Pop had nodded off. The radiation was taking its toll. It hit me yet again: my father was ill, he was

dying, and our tête-à-têtes that I cherished so, would one day cease to be.

Tears welled up in my eyes, as I placed a throw blanket over him, tucked a soft pillow under his head, kissed him on the forehead, and whispered, "I love you, Popsicle." I proceeded to the kitchen to tell Lessie Lee and the nurse to watch over him, that I would return in the morning.

Every time I walked out his front door it felt like an apocalyptic warning. I would take a moment to glance at the moon pasted in the evening sky, praying that throat cancer would not desecrate my father into a coma by morning. As I climbed my pregnant body into my car, I wondered if that would be the last time I would ever see Pop. But I did not want to invite that notion in. I trusted my father would stick it out long enough to see the birth of his grandchild. Nothing would keep him from that sacred moment, not even the grim reaper himself.

When I returned to my father's home the following day, I came with my husband, Guy Garner. Guy was six foot three inches, handsome and half Italian. Guy loved Dad as much as I did, and they were very close. They had often had "movie nights" together. Lessie Lee marched upstairs to the master bedroom to announce our arrival. She came out and motioned us up the stairs.

"What's up, Guy, getting taller?" My father joked, sitting up in bed. Guy smiled.

"Pop, Guy and I have something to tell you . . ." I said, choking up. Guy had to finish for me.

"Mr. D," he said, "we found out we are having a

boy. We decided to name our baby Sam, after you."

There was a moment of silence. Pop and I locked eyes. Then my father trembled, broke down, and burst into tears. "Thanks for my gift," he said in a soft whisper.

Guy and I went back downstairs so as not to cry convulsively in front of my father. By the time we got downstairs, my father's doctors had arrived. He asked to have a word with me outside.

Three doctors and Pop's assistant, Murphy, explained that my father would not be alive when our baby was born. I should not have any false hope. I knew they were trying to prepare me, but I didn't believe one word. I trusted God now. I trusted in the revelation that I would one day place Dad's newborn grandson in his lap.

One more thing, they added, your father wants you to be responsible for his wishes. *What wishes?* I thought. He is in so much pain, the doctors announced, we will have to up his morphine level, but it will ease out with the overloading—the morphine will eventually stop his heart.

I went back up to my father's bedroom, only to find his window wide open. Pop had overheard the doctor. He looked me straight in the eye and said, "I'm not going anywhere until I see my grandson. I'm staying around to see Sam. After that, I have nothing left to live for."

I kissed Dad on the forehead, and went back downstairs in tears. I trusted my father's determination and his will—more than the stinging words out of medical mouths.

I made the decision that today would not be a good day to reminisce with my father, given the emotional roller coaster we were all riding. I planned to revisit in the morning, open the four French doors off the living room to his emerald garden sanctuary, and take Pop out to drink in the air, sit, and talk.

Frank Sinatra was playing on the stereo in the living room when I returned in the morning. My father was on his Gucci half-moon couch resting. I opened the French doors out to the garden oasis. The nurse assisted my father outside. We sat on a couple of chaise lounges to take in the beauty of the outdoors. We listened faintly to Uncle Frank's music sent forth from the living room. Pop was happy I was there to tell his tales to, and I was delighted to hear him in good spirits, sharing monologues from his lips to my ears.

"The first time I met Frank Sinatra was in 1941 at the Michigan Theatre in Detroit," Pop said without skipping a beat.

"The Will Mastin Trio was replacing an act for three days and we opened for the Tommy Dorsey Orchestra and Frank. It was the swing era, Trace Face—the Stone Age to you. Frank and I shared a sandwich before showtime. I was the entertainer; Frank was the voice."

I added, "Uncle Frank may have been the voice, Pop, but he was also the agitator! You were the go-to-hell guy! Uncle Dean was the make-it-work gentle kind of soul. He seemed to soften everybody up like a Downy sheet in a dryer."

Pop could often be found with a camera in hand. Here he is during rehearsals of a Mastin Trio performance.

"True, Trace, but that was later, in the Vegas days. Back in 1941, it was just me and Frank, the entertainer and the voice. We bonded that day at the Michigan Theatre, talking shop."

"Soul brothers for life," I said. Comedian and actor Pat Cooper told documentarians Sacher and Langer that, "Nobody but Frank Sinatra could have put Sammy Davis where he was. Sinatra, first of all, was never a racist kind of a guy. He cared about everybody being equal. . . . When Frank said, 'This guy's great'—they all paid attention."

Pop told his story about Uncle Frank: "I remember how Frank used to study Dorsey—examine him like some specimen," Pop said. "Frank noticed how Dorsey snuck in breaths through an air hole in the side of his mouth while playing the trombone. Frank said he wanted to use that technique to hold his notes longer, keep a stanza going without having to stop for air. Frank's vocal range was outstanding, smooth, romantic, and rich with nuance. Never occurred to us back in the day that moons later we would be living in the limelight as the Rat Pack in Vegas," Pop explained.

"In 1947, we worked the Capitol Theatre in New York. We both had a three-week engagement. We were inseparable. Oh how Uncle Frank would woo those girls with his sultry love songs. Trace Face, girls were screaming from that electric aura that was Sinatra, swooning in lines for autographs."

"What was your role in the Tommy Dorsey show, Pop?"

"I featured impressions of celebrity singers in the opening act. Uncle Frank always encouraged me to sing in my own voice. He was right, in the long run. After the Michigan Theatre, Uncle Frank became a lifelong soul mate and best man at my wedding to your mother," Pop said.

"Mom must have taken your breath away in that beautiful wedding dress!" I said.

"My heart jumped out of its rib cage every time I cast my eyes on your mom. Everyone said, 'May Britt had a face chiseled like a Swedish goddess.' Her beauty, her grace, that 'interracial' wedding, now that's a story for another day! But as for Uncle Frank, he did stand up as my best man, was and always will be the best friend I ever had, truly."

I could tell all the reminiscing had sucked the wind out of Pop. His eyes were starting to droop. I handed him a throw blanket and said, "Here, Pop, why don't you catch yourself a little nap."

"You'll be here when I wake, Trace Face?"

"Perhaps in the powder room, baby is sitting on my bladder."

Pop smiled, closed his eyes, and nodded off in his sacred outdoor sanctuary. I made my pregnancy stop to the powder room, returned to sit by Pop, and watch him sleep, so at peace.

As I gazed out at his lavish Beverly Hills estate, I was beaming with pride at all my father had accomplished in life. I wondered if I would ever be that successful. Flashes of stories my father had shared when he first started making money consumed my mind.

One story that always made me smile was at the Roadhouse in Waterford, Connecticut, in the early 1940s. Pop and Burt and Jane Boyar wrote about it in his autobiography, *Yes I Can*. A half-dollar flew toward Pop, a teenager, onstage. He danced to it, picked it up, flipped it in the air, caught it, and put it in his pocket without losing a beat. The audience cheered, and suddenly it started to rain money. Dad was so weighted down by coins in his pocket he could barely dance through the closing act. He was living his dream.

But money didn't always buy happiness. Pop was a fish out of water with kids his own age. He was the oddball, the misfit, didn't know the first thing about real life.

My mom had a glamorous career in movies before she met my dad. She was touted as a "new" Swedish goddess in the style of Greta Garbo.

One time he was in a candy store in Harlem in the 1940s. Some of his peers were trading baseball cards. Pop didn't have a clue what a baseball card was since he was on the stage since the age of three, performing vaudeville instead of going to school. The kids started taunting Pop, humiliating him. My father tried to impress his peers by buying ten packs of baseball cards, a hundred in all. But the kids continued to laugh at him when he traded away his top players. That day, Pop ran home to Mama, and cried himself to sleep.

Years later, after all of Harlem knew he was a rising star, my father bumped into those same peers at the same candy shop. This time they all wanted his autograph. Just like Pop, he never held a grudge. He smiled, signed their autographs, and killed 'em with kindness. Pop had style and class. He also had the attitude of "You think I can't do this? Done. And watch out, folks, because one day I will buy and sell your sorry butts."

My grandfather and Uncle Will always tried to shield Pop, at least in his early years, from any form of hatred from his peers or the public. His father would explain away slights and snubs as sheer jealousy. They were determined to free Pop from the limitations of prejudice, particularly the racial ignorance heavily prevalent back in the day.

Pop's first real taste of racial injustice was at El Rancho Hotel in Las Vegas in the 1940s. It's torn down now but it opened big on April 3, 1941, on the southwest corner of Las Vegas Boulevard and Sahara. For a time it was the largest hotel in Las Vegas, with 110 rooms.

The Will Mastin Trio was pulling in $500 a week for their act, but the hotel would not allow "colored" entertainers to book a room, or even use the dressing rooms. The Mastin Trio had to wait out by the swimming pool between acts. Colored people could not gamble in the casinos, dine, or drink in the hotel restaurants and bars. House rules always sent the trio to the west side of Vegas to a colored boarding house.

The "colored" boarding house was a shack made of wooden crates run by a landlady named Ms. Cartwright. Ms. Cartwright capitalized on the fact that her boarding house was the only place in town colored entertainers could stay in Vegas. She charged a fortune for a room, twice as much as a room at El Rancho Hotel, with one perk—she would press your clothes.

Pop would ask his father, "Why are we staying here?" His father, relentlessly shielding young Sammy from racial adversity, would simply tell Pop the same ole line, "Oh hell, son, they're just jealous of our act."

Pop would later recount in a 1989 interview on Terry Wogan's BBC show that "in the '50s, every black star that worked Vegas, that helped build it up, who would pack a joint—I'm talking Lena Horne, Nat King Cole, Billy Eckstine, the Mills Brothers—were not allowed to eat there, could not walk through the front door of the casino, gamble, nothing. You would perform, get out of the casino by the side door, and head to the ghetto."

Claude Trenier said, "I remember an incident at the Riviera. Billy Eckstine went in there—he and his manager—at the craps table, and the guy says, 'You can't play. We don't serve niggers here.' Billy Eckstine socked him right in his jaw. Oh, we ran into that quite a bit . . . we had to go out and sit out by the swimming pool until our next appearance. They didn't have dressing rooms or nothing for us. When we lived here, we had to go on the west side—to the colored boarding house."

Many years later, once Pop's eyes were opened to the real sign of the times, he refused to entertain at places that practiced racial discrimination. He made certain it was in his contract that the trio would be allowed room, board, full use of the facilities, and would permit colored people in his audience. But he always had mixed emotions about that.

"By integration we lost a great deal and we gained a great deal," Pop told Terry Wogan. "When everything started to integrate, in terms of acceptance . . . we lost the ghetto, which was all our culture. There was the colored barbershop, and I say 'colored' because that was the terminology used in those days. The 'colored' rooming house where we all stayed, there was community. We all suffered the same indignities; it brought us, as black performers, closer together. We shared experiences and we hung out. As soon as it started to open up, and everyone could stay at the hotel they were working in, we very rarely saw each other anymore. And it's a shame we lost that; it's too bad we couldn't have maintained a little balance."

Unfortunately, during World War II, my father no longer had my grandfather and Uncle Will to protect and shelter him from the racial injustice in the army. In 1943, my father joined the Infantry Basic Training Center at Fort Francis E. Warren in Cheyenne, Wyoming.

My father was a gun enthusiast and an avid movie nut. He pictured himself as an aerial gunner in the Air Corps, a little guy in a cockpit with his scarf blowing in the wind, shooting at the enemy like in some old Hollywood movie. But Pop never had any schooling, so when he took his exams for the Air Corps, it was clear that he couldn't write and could barely read. He could not join the only black unit, the Tuskegee Airmen, as they had graduated with the highest honors.

Dad was sent to the Infantry Basic Training Center. The infantry of his dreams it was not. But at least he didn't have to read and write. My father was a patriot and agreed to defend his country. What he did not expect was to defend himself against enemies within his own military unit—bigots in his own barracks. It turned out to be an awakening he would never forget.

"What are you up to, Pregasaurus?" Pop woke from his power nap.

"Just watching you nap, Pop. Brain cells churning . . . ," I said.

"What's on your mind, Trace Face?"

In the army Dad learned to use his talent as a weapon against racial prejudice.

Frank Sinatra may have been King of the Bobbysoxers in the 1940s, but Dad made some young female fans of his own.

"I was thinking about the time you were in the army," I explained.

"Been there, done that!" Pop said.

"Stories, Pop, I want to hear the stories . . . again!" I begged. I wanted to hear it from the horse's mouth, not just read about it in his interviews and books.

"Awwww, grab me another Strawberry Crush and maybe I'll indulge you but keep in mind,

viewer discretion is advised!"

I smiled and went inside to the bar. The nurse handed me pills for my father to take with his Strawberry Crush. I placed his drink and pills next to his chaise lounge out by his sacred garden and pool. He swallowed the pills as I sat next to him.

"Your turn," I said to my father.

"Well, Trace Face, I was seventeen when I joined the army, all of five foot six inches and one hundred twenty pounds. All the soldiers were twice my size. A little lost, I politely ask a white PFC sitting on the barracks' steps where Building Two Hundred Two was located. He sized me up and down, reluctantly told me it is two buildings down followed by 'And I'm not your buddy, you black bastard!'"

"What an entrance you made, Pop. Dignity down the drain."

"Overnight the world was different. It wasn't one color anymore. The protection I'd gotten from my father and Uncle Will was a farce. I appreciated their loving hope to shield me from prejudice, hate, bigotry—but they were wrong. It was as if I'd walked through a swinging door for seventeen years, a door which they had always secretly held open," Pop explained.

"I realized then that you can pass legislation for desegregation, but you can't legislate people's minds. It's like hacking off the top of a weed: After we do it, we've got to get down and pull out the roots, get to the heart of the ignorance and intolerance, so it won't keep growing," Pop said.

"When I arrived at Unit Barracks Two Hundred Two, a corporal checked my name off his clipboard and told me to wait on the sidelines until they 'figure out what to do with me.' White kids showed up, simply walked inside and took the first bunk they saw. Another colored kid, tall, with his gear, was sent to sit on the side by me. We shook hands. His name was Edward. We both knew trouble was stirring."

"So what happened, Pop?" I asked.

"Felt like a lifetime that me and this colored kid waited outside the barracks watching the last white kid march in. We sat outside a screen door, as we were ordered."

"We could hear the corporal address the unit. He said, 'Folks, we got a problem, we got niggers outside assigned to this company. I'll stick 'em down there, but move your gear so I can give 'em the last two bunks.'"

"Then one of the guys piped up, 'Hey, that's right next to me! I ain't sleepin' next to no dinge!' The corporal made it clear who was in charge of the unit, but the same guy kept mouthing off, 'I'm only sayin' I didn't join no nigger army,'" Pop recalled.

"All the guys started shouting about how they ain't sharing no toilet can with no nigger, and what the hell's the army need 'em niggers for, just to steal us blind while we sleep? The corporal quieted them down with a simple, 'Knock it off. I don't want 'em anymore than you do, but we're stuck with 'em. That's orders,'" Pop said.

"The corporal motioned us in with our gear 'on the double.' My legs were shaking, trembling. As he

To the delight of thousands, Dad performed at Lankenheath Air Base in 1960. This was a far cry from the performances he did while in the army himself during World War II.

Years after the humiliation and discrimination of his experiences at Fort Francis, my father was warmly received on military bases as a superstar.

marched us down the aisle—eyes glaring on either side of us—soldiers guarded their cots spaced about three feet apart. The corporal pointed to the last two beds on one side, separated from the rest by about six feet with one empty cot between us and the white soldiers. It was as if we had the plague and were being quarantined."

"A sergeant marched in. He announced his name, Sergeant Williams. He glanced at the space between the beds. He gave a cold stare to the corporal and said, 'What the hell is that?' The corporal whispered quietly to the sergeant about how he was trying to deal with the nigger problem."

"Sergeant Williams was fuming, 'There is only one way we do things here and that is the army way! You have sixty seconds to replace the beds with exactly three feet of space, to the inch, between every cot in this barracks. Move!' For a brief moment, I felt safe."

"Sergeant Williams asked us questions: When did we arrive? How long did it take for us to get our bunks? Did you choose your bunks? Then the sergeant told us to move our gear one bunk closer to the white soldiers. He addressed the whole unit, 'No man here is better than the next man unless he's got the rank to prove it!'"

"I remember years later, George Rhodes, my conductor and arranger, told me he was surprised that with all the racial tension I endured, I never turned around and hated right back. I think that was because when I reached out for help, there was always some white guy like Sergeant Williams or

Frank Sinatra, who helped me back up. The black press would scrutinize me for it, but believe me, those cats saved the day for me."

"Sergeant Williams sounds like a good man, Dad," I said.

"From then on, I knew as long as Sergeant Williams was around we 'colored' folks would be safe," Pop added.

"But the minute the sergeant left, the soldiers tried to turn us into their slaves—making us polish their boots and such. I refused to do it and was teased as the 'uppity nigger boy.' Edward on the other hand, was not going to put up a fight for his own dignity, and I had no right to judge his desire to hide his pain. 'Yes, suh!' said Edward, 'Glad t'do 'em, suh.' I felt like I was on an island all alone," explained my father.

"Pop, I can't even imagine the horror of it all. How you lifted yourself up out of that muck and survived it is unfathomable!" I said.

"That's only the prelude to the circus act. Your grandfather had given me an expensive one hundred twenty–buck gold watch to take with me to the army. I treasured it. The white soldiers got a hold of my watch on the first day in the barracks. They tossed it back and forth to each other, over my head, laughing as I chased after it. You know how little I was—still am! These white cats were huge.

"Eventually, Jennings, the biggest bigot of them all, ground my watch into the floor with the heel of his boot. He crushed the glass, twisted the gold, and broke the hands off. It was mangled in pieces. I

picked up the remains, went to my bed, and wrapped it in paper. Jennings shouted behind me, 'You can always steal another, nigger boy!' The whole incident crushed me, deeply," Pop said solemnly.

"How does somebody do that to someone?" I was disgusted.

"Because they can, because they *could*, back in the day. Every night I would lay in bed, wondering what is it about skin that made people hate so much. But it was far deeper than skin; to these white cats, I was a different breed," my father explained.

"I had to face the fact that the army vultures were going to prey on me daily. Try to eat me alive. I thought of my father, Uncle Will, the agents, the managers, the acts we worked with—nobody treated us this way. Or had my father just shielded me from it all? I knew we stayed in colored boarding houses made of wooden crates, but I didn't realize we *had* to stay there. My father said we stayed there because people were . . ."

". . . jealous of our act?" I replied.

"That's right. And somehow, in my naïve, sheltered world, I believed it. All I knew was that when the Will Mastin trio got onstage, people laughed, clapped, were entertained. Talent earned us respect," my father said.

"Talent shielded you," I told Dad.

"Talent was my only weapon. Eventually in the army, I was transferred to an entertainment regiment in an 'experimental' integrated Special Services unit. But until that transfer, Sergeant Williams got me a few gigs at the service club, thinking it might help," said Pop.

"After one show, Jennings appeared to be offering me his friendship. He handed me a beer. 'C'mon over here, Davis, let's get acquainted.' He pulled out a chair for me. 'You notice I ain't calling you 'boy.' I thought my talent finally broke the ice. But sure enough as I picked up the bottle of beer, I realized it was warm, not cold. I smelled it. Jennings had replaced my bottle of beer with urine."

Tears welled up in my eyes, then rolled down my cheek. It was just too overwhelming to hear. My father grabbed my hand. "Don't cry, Trace Face. I only tell you these stories so you will understand firsthand the adversity our race endured. It only made me stronger."

"Did Jennings and his guys ever let up, Pop?" I said choked up.

One hundred and twenty pounds was Dad's "fighting weight."

"Nah. I had a knock-down, drag out fight every two days. I can't even count how many times I was in the infirmary for a broken nose. When we finished basic training, my physical turned me down, and I was put through basic again. I didn't qualify for any of the army's specialist schools because I had no education at all," my father said.

"Sergeant Williams was my savior. He would call me into his office to offer his advice. 'You've got to fight with your brains, Sammy, not your fists.' Sergeant Williams told me I had to stop looking at comic books and learn to read. He taught me to read and write. God bless that man."

"The first book I ever read was *The Three Musketeers*. Long, thick, and let me tell you, I am never going to read it again. But Sergeant Williams had me read all the classics. He would select books from Dickens to Twain to Abraham Lincoln, even *The Complete Works of Shakespeare*. I would circle the words I didn't know. He would sit in the squad room at the end of the barracks and explain it to me. Sergeant Williams gave me hope that I could overcome this battle, Trace."

"What you put in your mind, no one can take away from you, right, Pop?" I said.

"Listen to you, the philosopher! The latrine became my temple. I would read religiously after taps in that dimly lit latrine, and report back to Sergeant Williams. We would have our own civilized discourse on each book. I hungered for that time with him. He made me feel like a human being again. His office became my own sacred refuge, a retreat from the racism, hate, ignorance, and intolerance of my unit."

"What became of Sergeant Williams, Pop?"

"I don't know. But I owe him my life. He tempered all the humiliation I felt from my unit. He distracted me from all my rage, all my anger. I wouldn't have survived the army without him," my father replied.

"The last straw with Jennings was the worst of all. After I did a little Frank Sinatra number at the Officers' Club, impressing a general, word was out that I might be able to transfer into the integrated Special Services unit. There I could perform on a professional level for the entertainment regiment. Jennings wasn't pleased. He thought I was kissing butt to escape his abuse. I had to work out a budget for scenery, props, and costumes for a white female captain. This didn't sit well with Jennings. The captain had all the power to give me something to offer the army: my talent," Dad said.

"I can't imagine what Jennings did next," I replied.

"It was unimaginable, Trace," my father said with disgust. "Jennings and his gang jumped me on the way to a meeting with the captain. They cornered me, dragged me into a latrine, and beat the crap out of me."

"Oh, Pop," I said, holding back the tears.

"But that wasn't the worst of it. They took a can of white paint and wrote the word 'NIGGER' on my chest. They beat me until I was bleeding from every part of my body. I thought my life was done—I was going to be beaten to death. Just to add some icing on the cake, Jennings ended his circus act with, 'Now be a good little coon and give us a dance.'"

"Dear Lord, did you dance for him?" I asked.

"I danced for my life, Trace. After Jennings finished his finale, I wanted to crawl into the walls of the latrine and die. I thought to myself, I joined the Unites States Army to fight the enemy in whatever country at whatever time, but I never thought I would be sleeping with the enemy in my own unit, my own barracks."

"Did they transfer you after that nightmare, Pop?"

"Luckily, yes—into the entertainment regiment. I was able to perform to larger crowds, even got cheers from those who previously mistreated me. Prejudiced white men admired and respected my performances. I saw Jennings in the audience once. He didn't crack a smile, but I could tell from his expression I had won the battle, maybe not the war, but that battle. The spotlight lessened the prejudice. For me, it was a revelation. My talent was the weapon, the power, the way for me to fight. It was the one way I might hope to affect a man's thinking. From then on, deep in my heart, soul, and spirit, I knew I had to be a star."

"What about Grandpa and Uncle Will, did you tell them about the beatings in the army?" I asked my father.

"Not a word. My father and Uncle Will met me at the station in Los Angeles after I was discharged. After hugs and all that good stuff, my father noticed my treasured gold watch he had gifted me was not on my wrist. I just couldn't bear to tell him the truth. Why would I put my father and Uncle Will through the pain and suffering of hearing stories about prejudice, beatings, and white paint smearing the word 'NIGGER' across my chest? I told my father 'the watch got smashed on maneuvers.' Luckily, he believed me."

"That's so sad, Pop," I said.

"Heck. The army was in the past—history—and it was time to move into the future. I wanted to become a star, a shining star, a shooting star, a megastar, a legendary star—any kind of star would do. I needed to perform, entertain, sing, and dance. I was filled with sheer strength and determination to succeed, triumph, win the day."

"So there we are standing in the Los Angeles station. I am discharged from the army, free at last. I ask my father the same question I always asked him as a kid: 'Where we goin', Dad?' The melody of his refrain was music to my ears when I heard him exclaim, 'We're going back into show business, son!' And off we went, full speed ahead."

Once Dad's star was on the ascent, nothing could stop him.

CHAPTER 2

BREAKTHROUGH

After the car accident in which he lost an eye, Dad often posed with
more of the right side of his face showing. This is him in 1958.

It was an early spring afternoon when I got a call from Shirley Rhodes, my father's assistant/manager since before I was born. Shirley was the wife of George Rhodes, my father's beloved musical director for thirty years. "Your father's in the hospital, you better come now," Shirley announced. I thought my heart would stop.

I waddled down the hall, my pregnant belly bursting into the celebrity suites at Cedars-Sinai Medical Center in Los Angeles. I entered the outer chamber to the Sammy Davis, Jr. suite.

"How's Dad?" I asked Shirley. "Is he getting better?"

"Not exactly, sweetie." Shirley prepped me: It turned out Pop's second radiation treatment did not work. He was not in remission at all. The doctors were starting him on chemotherapy through an IV and fighting some other infection that was ravaging his body. "And don't be alarmed, they have a trachea tube down his throat. He can't speak unless he holds his hand over the trach hole," said Shirley.

How could this be? I thought to myself. What kind of quagmire was this? I remembered the fights I had with my father when he was first diagnosed with throat cancer. I wanted him to have surgery, cut out the tumor. The doctors said if they cut out the tumor he would lose his voice box. Pop refused to have the surgery. We had two options: surgery with a seven in ten chance to live, or radiation that gave him a three in ten chance to live. He would never, under any circumstance, have surgery and risk losing his singing voice. "It's my decision," he

kept telling me. Then there we were, two radiations and chemo later, and Pop has a trachea tube down his throat—his voice snatched from him anyway.

My father quite simply and honestly was scared when he was first diagnosed with cancer. He was scared to die, of course, but more scared to lose his gift: the Sammy Davis, Jr. voice, his God-given talent. That would bare him naked in a way. His talent, his voice, had gotten him where he was: 12,600 square feet smack in the middle of Beverly Hills, a lifetime of performing, dedication to charities, and still performing to packed houses. Without his voice, what would he have? He would be a superhero without a cape.

All I thought about was making certain that he would not die. Pop had us, his family, his friends, his fans, we all loved him and refused to live without him. Sam was going to be born, and Pop was determined to be the best grandfather ever. He was going to make up for lost time. He was going to learn to change diapers. All of the "regular" stuff parents and grandparents do every day. In short, my father was going to be "normal." Ha! What the heck was I thinking? Pop normal? Pop was anything but.

I truly believed the radiation would work. The doctor said he was getting better. Now he was worse. It was a race to the finish line—would Dad die first or would I have the baby first? Everyone thought giving birth to Sam was going to be the miracle cure. The pressure was incalculable. Sam

My "Pop," 1962

My father's identity was so completely tied up with his ability to perform. As I watched him grow more and more ill at the end of his life, my mind often drifted to scenes like this of him solo in the spotlight, 1961.

was safe and sound in my tummy, blissfully unaware of the tragedy that was unfolding each and every day. Thank God for that.

As for me, I had no idea if Sam would be the miracle cure. I vacillated back and forth, swinging like a pendulum. On the one hand, I was begging my obstetrician, Dr. Karalla, to take Sam out early, so Dad would get that chance to hold his grandson. On the other hand, I was afraid for my baby to be born, for fear that Pop would die shortly thereafter. It was the best of times and the worst of times.

Shirley snapped me out of my hole of despair with a big bear hug. She tried to cheer me up by showing me the myriad flowers and cards from fans, family, and friends that encompassed the outer room of Pop's private hospital suite.

Evidently, Denzel Washington had just left, having given my father a copy of his film, *Glory*. She mentioned that Bill Cosby, Eddie Murphy, Arsenio Hall, and a few other celebrities were planning to stop by to visit Pop in the next few days.

All I could think of was how much my father would hate having all those visitors. He liked to be seen in his glory, certainly not the way he was at the hospital.

A nurse came out of Pop's inner room, announced that he was sleeping, but I could go sit by him if I cared to. I was terrified to go in, panic-stricken that this could be the beginning of the end for Pop. But I took a deep breath, hoping it would send a message to my brain to calm down, stood valiantly tall, and walked in.

I was greeted by an ominous collection of tubes that were attached to my father like living, breathing parasites. He had a trachea tube protruding from his throat, an IV in his arm, and machines everywhere. As I pulled up a chair next to my father's bed, I noticed his face as he slept. It was hauntingly thin, but not quite as bad as I had expected. Unfortunately, the menacing odor from that tumor on his neck threatened to attack. During my pregnancy I was extremely sensitive to smell, and his tumor seemed to have a sinister odor all its own.

I picked up an old record a visitor had placed as a gift on a bed table next to him. It was one of the first singles Pop ever released, "The Way You Look Tonight."

After my father was released from the army, he rejoined the family dance act, playing around the country, being singled out and praised by critics. Late in 1948, Dad was on a radio broadcast from Los Angeles and was overheard by Capitol Records executive Dave Dexter Jr. Dad signed a twenty-record deal at fifty bucks a side. The most successful single released was "The Way You Look Tonight." *Metronome* magazine chose it as the 1949 "Record of the Year" and named Dad the year's "Most Outstanding New Personality."

Even though he'd had his first hit, my dad was hoping for greater success with his first record label. He began working with David Cavanaugh—"Big

Dave"—at Capitol Records. Cavanaugh was known for composing, arranging, and producing records for my dad and others, including Frank Sinatra and Nat King Cole. At the age of twenty-three, on January 13, 1949, Pop undertook his first recording session for Capitol Records, starting with the songs "I Don't Care Who Knows," "The Way You Look Tonight," and "Please Don't Talk About Me When I'm Gone." Dad eventually recorded twenty sides for Capitol in 1949. It was not the successful turn he hoped for. Dad blamed his lack of success with Capitol on the poor arrangements of Cavanaugh, rather than the fact that he was just getting his foot in the door. According to music review journalist William Ruhlmann, "Sammy's Capitol material was more of the work of a young artist trying to find his voice and doing so by trying out various different approaches. Sometimes he sounds like other singers of the day, perhaps unintentionally; other times, he is deliberately doing impressions with comic intent." My father was clearly still finding his own voice—the one that would make him stand out from the crowd of stars.

In March 1951, my father got the praise he was seeking. It happened at Ciro's nightclub on the Sunset Strip in Los Angeles. Ciro's was packed with celebrities who had gathered after the Academy Awards. His much heralded performance at Ciro's that night led the family act to the hottest clubs across the country, including the Fairmont Hotel in San Francisco, the Beachcomber in Miami Beach, the Flamingo in Las Vegas, and the Riviera in New Jersey.

The Riviera is where Dad first met Morty Stevens, a clarinetist in the Riviera house band. Pop had been begging his father for his own arranger and conductor for years. Morty took the job and hit the road with my father. Morty later broke out on his own, winning two Emmys for composing the theme tune for *Hawaii Five-O*. Shirley's husband, George Rhodes, took over the job as Pop's musical arranger for thirty years. After George passed away, it devastated my father, and Morty came back again to arrange and conduct for Dad.

My father had an entourage of loyal, faithful staff—all turned into family members for life: Lessie Lee, Shirley and George Rhodes, Morty Stevens, Arthur Silber (his advisor and business partner for over twenty-five years), Charley, his driver, Murphy Bennett, his assistant, and others.

Frank Sinatra was his closest "lifelong" friend. He was a mentor when Pop was a teenager and his best friend until the day he died. Dad was "the Kid" to Frank; and later he affectionately called him "Smokey." Their relationship was a rare precious gem only they could touch. Pop had a heart of gold and was truly beloved by those who got close to him.

Pop started to stir in his bed. I heard a faint raspy whisper. I leaned my ear in toward his lips. He covered his hand over a hole in the trachea tube and spoke again, "Hey Trace Face you get uglier every time I see you."

"Hi, Pop," I said, holding back the tears.

Dad and the man he called his best friend, Frank Sinatra, in 1967.
Their friendship lasted more than forty years.

"I got this new gadget to play with, baby!" Pop tapped on his trachea tube.

"I see," I said, choking up.

"Where's that fine nurse?" Pop said, holding the trachea hole. I rang the buzzer for the nurse.

"Can I help you, Mr. Davis?" the nurse entered.

"I need to use the restroom," Pop said. The nurse proceeded to pull out a bedpan, politely motioning me to leave the room.

"Darling, I'm a superstar, get me up, I'm not going in a bedpan!" Dad exclaimed.

No, Pop was not going in a bedpan. My father created his own rules his whole life. He was a pioneer, consistently breaking the color barrier as an African American entertainer.

In 1953, ABC Television commissioned a $200,000-sitcom pilot starring "the Trio," as the Mastin Trio was commonly called. This was an unheard of achievement for a group of African Americans. The pilot was not picked up, but that did not stop Pop from flourishing in the world of television.

He was a guest on Eddie Cantor's *The Colgate Comedy Hour* and Ed Sullivan's *Toast of the Town.* Eddie Cantor and Pop were old friends and on the air Cantor had no qualms about showing off their friendship by hugging him and wiping my father's brow with his own handkerchief. NBC protested the

TOP: The Mastin Trio, led by my father.

BOTTOM: The Mastin Trio together in *Mr. Wonderful* on Broadway, 1956

The Mastin Trio marquee at the Apollo in New York, 1954

broadcast and threatened to pull their backing from the show. Cantor reacted by booking Pop for the rest of the season. God bless him.

By September 1954, Pop had found his singing voice thanks to a new recording contract with Decca Records, and his first single, "Hey There" climbed to #1 on the *Cashbox* record charts. The Trio headlined to rave reviews at the Copacabana in New York City the same year. Table by table at the Copa, the audience stood, clapped, roared, and demanded encores. It brought my grandpa, Uncle Will, and my father to tears right on the stage. On closing night, Pop gave the staff at the Copa gold watches engraved: THANKS, SAMMY DAVIS, JR. Pop was a bona fide class act.

The following day, the Trio, Mama, Morty, and Pop's entourage all headed to Hollywood to rent a house—no easy task given the racial tension of the day. No one wanted "niggers" as neighbors, even if they were superstars.

When the crew arrived in Los Angeles after their success at the Copa, my grandfather and Uncle Will bought my father a brand new Cadillac convertible to cruise around the Hollywood Strip in.

As tacky as it sounds, yes, the car had "SD Jr." painted on the door. My father told me and recounted in his autobiography, *Yes I Can*, that he would never forget the first time they all rode in that new Cadillac.

Pop was smoking like a chimney, filling up the ashtray, and said to his father and Uncle Will, "Hey, guys, what do we do when this thing gets filled up?"

His father smiled and said, "Son, we throws this car away and gets us a new one!" Uncle Will laughed and roared, "You boys keep up those old jokes and we'll be back riding in the back of the bus!"

After more than twenty years of performing, Pop was becoming a superstar.

Twenty-five or so years later, he was a superstar who was not going in a bedpan.

"God, I hate it here . . . ," Dad muttered as the nurse assisted him back into his hospital bed.

Pop always detested hospitals. It started from his 1954 nearly fatal car accident that took his left eye. During the mid-1970s, Pop's addictive lifestyle gave him liver and kidney trouble that sent him to the hospital for several months. Uncle Frank cut off his friendship with Dad for a short period to force him to clean up his act. Dad turned to cooking to fight his own addictions, and it worked. My father became a gourmet cook.

In 1974, Pop suffered a heart attack, but recovered and continued his relentless work pace. From 1975 to 1977, Pop hosted the television variety show *Sammy and Company*, performed in the Broadway musical *Stop the World—I Want to Get Off*, cut more singles, and continued to perform in casinos and nightclubs across the nation. Pop was back in the hospital in 1985, when he had reconstructive hip surgery (so he could dance again).

The hip recovery coincided with his birthday in December 1985, and the only thing that cheered Pop up was a letter from the President of the United States himself, Ronald Reagan. It read:

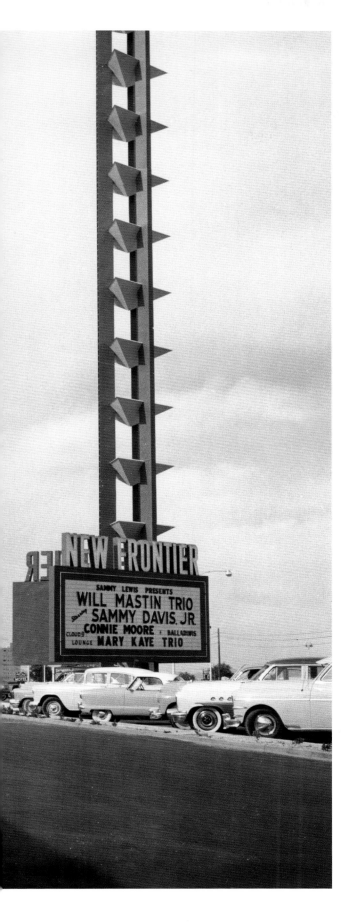

Dear Sammy,

Nancy and I understand that Altovise has planned a wonderful surprise birthday party for you. We send our warmest congratulations and our special hope that you are well along the road to recovery from your recent surgery.

If this occasion brings some reflection on your part you should have a fine time musing over the fullness of your life. From childhood on you have been a dynamic force in the entertainment industry. Whether it be singing, dancing or acting, you have done it with rare talent and dazzling energy. You have given audiences some of the finest performances they have ever seen. So, when you think about your accomplishments, don't forget all those fans— including Nancy and me—who are captivated and delighted by "Mr. Entertainment."

Happy birthday, Sammy, and may God bless and keep you.

Sincerely,
Ronald Reagan

Eventually the Will Mastin Trio became the "Will Mastin Trio—Starring Sammy Davis, Jr."

Now here he was back at Cedars-Sinai, in the hospital—with carcinoma growing behind his vocal cords. Pop was beyond ready to go home.

"Just think of it this way, Pop. Hospitals are one place where laziness is rewarded," I said.

"I was always lousy at being lazy . . . ," Pop replied.

"So your ex-wives claim." I chuckled.

"Heck, I've only had two so far! Loray [White, from 1958 to1959, a "proper" marriage to a black woman that diffused Dad's scandalous relationship with blonde superstar Kim Novak]—my dancer chic mistake, and [from 1960 to 1968] your blessed mother, May [Britt]." Dad grinned.

"And Altovise Gore. Oh, I'm sorry, Altovise *Davis* . . . when are you going to divorce that one?" I said.

"You are fierce, Trace Face. Divorce? And let her take half? Hell no. It's easier just to lock her out of the master wing of the house. Forget cancer, I'm more afraid of Altovise. If she got high enough, she could fall on me and kill me!" Pop laughed.

"I can see the headlines: Sammy Davis, Jr., crushed to death by drunken wife!" I said.

"That's the *New York Times* version. The *New York Post* would say, Entertainment's only black, Puerto Rican, one-eyed Jew crushed to death by drunken wife."

"Pop, Altovise only wants you because you made it," I told him.

"Made it? Me? I made it?" Dad chuckled.

"Seriously, Pop," I said.

"I did make it, didn't I? I'll never forget that time—the time I really knew in my heart that I had made it. It was November 1954. We headlined at the Frontier Casino in Las Vegas. What made it taste so sweet was the contract. The Trio pulled in $7,500 a week, but more importantly, our contract allowed us 'colored folks' to stay in the Frontier's best suites and have free run of the facilities—the casino, the restaurant, even the pool! All lodging, food, and drinks were free of charge. Beautiful!" Pop explained, hand over his trachea tube.

"Done with Ms. Cartwright and her colored boarding house across town, huh, Pop?" I asked.

"Done. Still mountains to climb, but we were making quantum leaps on both sides of the color spectrum. We were not a colored act or a white act, we were just an act. Huge crowds opened up for us as we walked through the front door, not the back door, mind you, of the Frontier. The sweet taste of freedom felt like stardom to us." Dad smiled with nostalgia in his eyes.

"It was a landmark achievement, Pop," I replied.

"Yes, it was. Doors were swinging open for us. Until I made that late night trip to Los Angeles . . ." Pop's smile turned on me.

"The car crash. Your eye," I said softly.

"You know the story, Tracey, and I am in no mood to repeat it!" When Pop said "Tracey" as opposed to Trace Face or Trace, I knew it was firm and serious.

"Where's that *Glory* film Denzel gave you?" I said, trying to move on.

"Ask Shirley," Pop said.

I went out to the outer chamber to retrieve *Glory* from Shirley. I brought it back and slipped it into the VCR. It was about time my dad rested his strained voice, anyway. I propped the pillow behind Pop's back and sat down on the bedside next to him. He grabbed my hand as the film started to roll.

I could not focus on *Glory*. My mind was on the car crash that took my father's eye the moment he got to revel in the adulation he strove so hard to win.

The car accident happened on November 19, 1954. Fans roared as my father exited the Frontier stage. "Make room for Sammy, Swinging Show, Sammy"—voices echoed in the halls as he headed up to his suite to pack a few items for Los Angeles. He called his driver, Charley, and told him, "No party tonight, we have to drive to Los Angeles." After showering, he put on a pair of Levi's and a sweater, packed casual items for his trip, and called room service for a burger.

What knocked on his door a short while later was not room service at all, but a chorus girl who motioned him straight into the bedroom. He went with the flow, but would have preferred the burger, he later said.

Charley was waiting in the car as my father climbed in the backseat. It was late. Pop watched the neon lights flash his name on the Frontier marquee as they drove off. The taste was sweet. Looking back at the marquee he knew a new era had opened up for him: success.

Dad once told me when we were sitting out on

Dad's pictured here wearing the mezuzah given to him by Eddie Cantor—it was Pop's "good luck charm."

Dad on his TV show in 1966,
embodying his nickname—
"Mr. Entertainment."

his patio that "Hey There" was playing on the radio the night of the car accident. Dad said he was listening to himself on the radio thinking it can't get better than this. There he was, headlining at the Frontier, listening to his own #1 single on the radio. Dare he dream for more?

He told his driver, "Keep it under fifty, Charley. Let's break this car in so smooth that she'll sing ballads," Pop said, unaware that a star was born and would nearly die the same night.

Not yet a Jew, Pop had received a gift of a mezuzah from Eddie Cantor. Pop used it not as a traditional blessing over a door, but wore it around his neck like a good luck charm. The only time Pop did not wear it out, was that night of the car crash.

Dad reached around his neck for the mezuzah, but it wasn't there. He couldn't recall taking it off at the Frontier, but with the frenzy of packing and the chorus chick frolicking about, it must have slipped off his neck. He thought about returning to retrieve it, but Charley was already twenty minutes away. It was late and they had a long drive ahead of them to Los Angeles. Dad opened his backseat window, and let the stars and clear desert breeze lull him to sleep.

The car crashed in San Bernardino, California, at a fork in US Highway 66 at Cajon Boulevard and Kendall Drive. A woman driving ahead on the highway got off at an exit, only to realize that it was the wrong exit. Dad had taken over in the driver's seat by this time. The lady backed up from the exit ramp onto the highway, and that's when the collision happened. Dad slammed his eye on the pointed cone in the middle of his steering wheel. The last thing he remembered was reaching for his left eye that was dangling out of its socket.

Dad woke up in the Community Hospital of San Bernardino, in total darkness, bandaged up like an Egyptian mummy. The impact fractured the bones of his face. His mind raced. He heard the random cacophony of hospital staff rushing in and out of his room. He felt the warm breeze of an open window; it felt like day, but it was pitch black. What time was it? He felt iron bars under his hands and realized he was strapped like a prisoner to the hospital bed. Was he paralyzed? His heart beat violently, throbbing with terror and fear. He moved his legs under the bed sheets, relieved to find he had working legs and feet.

But why was it so dark? Where was the sunlight? Was he blind? Would he live like a madman in the dark for the rest of his life? More terrible still was his imagination that plunged him into a deeper abyss of uncertainty: Would he ever perform again? Was God punishing him for becoming a star? Had he lost his way along the path to stardom, forsaken some moral, some principle, some holy commandment that forced God to take his sight from him? What was happening here? He yelled out, "Help me!"

A nurse rushed into the room and removed his hand restraints, telling Pop not to touch the bandages over his eyes. She told him that he was in a nearly fatal car accident, but he was going to be fine.

Fine? Dad felt his head. He felt no skin, just ominous bandages. His head hurt as he lay in the dark. He was not fine. My father pleaded with the

January 1955: In rehearsals for his return to performing at Ciro's in Hollywood after losing an eye in a car accident. Will Mastin is behind him.

Dad's first public performance, at Ciro's, after his car accident. You can see Dick Powell and June Allyson at a front table in this photo.

nurse to tell him if he was going to be blind. He would rather die at that very moment than live blind. The nurse simply replied that he was not going to be blind, and that he needed to rest. Pop knew the nurse would not be the one to break it to him; he would have to wait for the doctor, so he demanded the nurse page the doctor.

Within minutes, my father heard the heavy footsteps of a man entering his room. He introduced himself as Dr. Hull. In a solemn and gentle tone, the surgeon announced that he operated on my father the night before and was forced to remove his left eye.

What? Just like that, so matter of fact, he removed his left eye? My father touched his bandages, thinking perhaps he hadn't heard the doctor correctly. Pop grabbed for the bars on his hospital bed, steadying himself from the nausea of what he just heard. The horror of it all scared him beyond comprehension—it was an insidious and brutal entrapment.

TOP: Dad had many supporters in Hollywood after his comeback. Here he is with James Cagney.

BOTTOM: With Milton Berle

Dad shot a myriad of questions at the surgeon. Dr. Hull explained that he was a vision specialist called in to advise the doctors on duty struggling to save his eye after the crash. There was, at best, 10 percent vision possible for the left eye. However, as an expert in his field, he felt the strain on the healthy right eye would weaken both and result in "sympathetic blindness," that over a few years would result in total blindness. There was no choice but to remove his left eye, and once healed, replace it with an artificial eye that he would have to wear for life.

Questions flooded my father's mind: Was this man serious? An artificial eye? Jeopardize his new stardom? Would he dance again? What about his balance on the stage? Who would do the show at the Frontier while he was recovering in the hospital? All his dreams came to a halt as he scrambled to make sense of it all in the dark. His cry for answers was primal. He demanded the right to dignity, to work—nothing else, nothing more—just to work.

As my father convalesced, Frank Sinatra and others came by to console him. Flowers and cards from fans poured in. Dad's friend, actor Jeff Chandler, offered one of his own eyes if it would keep Pop able to perform. But medically, there was nothing to be done. Pop would have to wear an eye

Pop joining the party after a performance with the Will Mastin Trio.

patch for at least six months and later be fit with an artificial eye that he would wear from then on. As an entertainer, my father would have to master a balancing act with one eye, so as not to dance right off the stage.

As my father recovered from the removal of his left eye at the Community Hospital of San Bernardino back in 1954, he did a lot of deep and painful self-analysis about his rise to stardom. He examined his belief systems, his needs, desires, and

ABOVE: With Jack Carter in *Mr. Wonderful*, Dad's
first Broadway show

RIGHT: My father and Eartha Kitt in *Anna Lucasta*, 1958

the undercurrent of his own human spirit.

He dwelled on the fact that the only time he did not wear his mezuzah from Eddie Cantor was the night of the car accident. It turns out it had fallen behind the hotel bed before he left for the drive to Los Angeles. He didn't even realize at the time that a mezuzah was not traditionally worn around the neck, but the self-scrutiny of not wearing his "good luck charm" was enough to trigger my father to meet with a rabbi in the hospital.

My father's family was Baptist and until the accident he had not paid religion much thought. As my father spoke with the rabbi, he was enlightened by the abundance of spiritual and historical parallels between his own embattled identity as an African American and the oppression of the Jews. He learned that Judaism taught justice for everyone, particularly those who had been oppressed for centuries. It gave Pop an exhale of "I get this, I am a part of this."

A year later, in one of the first satellite interviews on the *Edward R. Murrow Show*, Pop said that the accident made him a better person, that it was the best thing that ever happened to him. Maybe an odd thing to say, but as a rising entertainer, doors opened up for him, and he got wrapped up in himself prior to the accident. He came to the realization that there were more important things than stardom—essential fellow goodness, generosity, kindness. His friends rallied around him and supported him through his recovery.

In the hospital, from his conversations and readings with the rabbi, Dad discovered more similarities that Jewish and black cultures both faced. Dad learned that in the early twentieth century, Jewish publications spoke of violence against blacks, and often compared the black racism in the South to *pogroms*, the violent mob attacks against Jews.

Dad also discovered that Jews played a major role in the founding of the NAACP in 1909. Dad learned that leaders in the American Jewish community used their economic resources, time, and energy to fight for black civil rights. The more he read, the deeper his conviction became to become Jewish.

Dad made his final decision to convert to Judaism after the hospital rabbi gave him Paul Johnson's *A History of the Jews* to read. One passage hit

home with Pop: *"The Jews would not die. Three centuries of prophetic teaching had given them an unwavering spirit of resignation and had created in them a will to live which no disaster could crush."*

My father never allowed himself to stay in a gloomy reality for long, no dark clouds over his head. Pop recovered from the 1954 car crash at Frank's place in Palm Springs. Frank drove seventy miles to bring my father to his home to recuperate and get his stride back. Frank was determined not to let his handicap stop him from being a star. Pop's talent was once again his weapon, the only way out of this madness. He wore his eye patch for at least six months and almost fell off the stage a few times, but eventually learned to keep his balance again as he danced. He even appeared on *What's My Line?* wearing the patch.

He was fitted with an artificial eye and rolled on to become a bona fide star. Pop always combatted horror with humor, and continued to joke onstage about being the only "black, Puerto Rican, one-eyed Jewish Entertainer" in the world.

In 1954, the same year as the accident, Pop sung the title track for the Universal Pictures film *Six Bridges to Cross*. In April 1955, my father's first LP, *Starring Sammy Davis, Jr.* rose to #1 on the charts.

Mr. Wonderful was a musical comedy written specifically to showcase my father's talents as a Las Vegas nightclub entertainer. The story focused on

Dad singing his heart out in *Porgy and Bess*, 1959

the entertainer Charlie Welch's struggles in the industry. The cast brought together the Will Mastin Trio, and Sammy recorded a sixteen-track vocal jazz album highlighting the staged play.

Mr. Wonderful opened on March 22, 1956 at the Broadway Theater, closing on February 23, 1957 after 383 grueling performances. Joseph Stein and Will Glickman were the authors of the original book upon which the musical was based. The music and lyrics were composed by George David Weiss, Jerry Bock, and Larry Holofcener.

Pop was back with a vengeance. He even hit the big screen in movies like *Anna Lucasta* and *Porgy and Bess*. By 1959, he was about to take over Las Vegas with the baddest and coolest cats in entertainment history, better known as the Rat Pack. But that was a story for another visit with Dad.

After Pop's accident and his conversion to Judaism, there were fans who supported his decision to become a Jew, and some members of the Jewish and African American communities that would not embrace him. But it made no difference to my father; he had fought bigger battles in his life.

Pop always took the road less traveled, the road that takes you to the heart of human understanding, generosity, and fellowship. In Pop's view, Jews and blacks not only shared a history of oppression, but were all related as seen by their darker complexions and curly hair from Northern Africa, Egypt, Israel, and neighboring countries. Why not embrace his own race as well as Judaism? In the Davis family, that is what we did.

My mother, Swedish actress May Britt, converted to Judaism before she even married my dad. The Davis family would be raised Jewish. Every Friday night we would celebrate the Sabbath at sundown with my mother. We had a nonsecular Christmas tree, simply because my mom liked to decorate it.

Our summer vacations were spent in Lake Tahoe, where Dad would perform at Harrah's or in Reno. After their divorce, my mother moved us to Lake Tahoe permanently, and she continued to raise us Jewish. There was no Jewish community or even temple at the time in Lake Tahoe. We would travel over an hour away, to Reno, just to attend temple, go to Hebrew school—or to see Pop's show. My brother, Mark, had a bar mitzvah, and we would celebrate the traditional Jewish holidays like Hanukkah and Passover with friends. We built our own little Jewish community in Lake Tahoe led by Dr. Phillip Charney, a Jewish dermatologist turned rabbi who graciously opened his home to us.

The Davis family were Jews, period. Well, except for Mom's soul food cooking! Not exactly kosher. Despite Pop's best efforts—my Swedish mom had no rhythm, wasn't very musical, and was always off-beat. Mom remembered being at Pop's show at the Sands, the whole audience was clapping in rhythm, then came one off-beat single clap. Pop stopped the orchestra and said, "That must be my wife!" He got a big roar of laughter that night. Now as for her soul food attempt, as told to me by my mother:

Mom said they we are in Lake Tahoe—for the family it was a summer getaway, although Pop, of course, was working. He was performing at Harrah's, for his lifelong friend Bill Harrah. At the time, early '60s or so, Harrah's Hotel area was pretty barren, so they built a little place just for entertainers. It had a small kitchenette, with three burners, no oven. Mom got this idea that she would make soul food. Loving to cook and born in Harlem, Pop gave her some simple soul food tips—*simple* being the key word. Mother decided she was going to master this. Good Lord!

Mother called the local Tahoe town market, "This is Mrs. Sammy Davis, Jr. I need pig tails." Dead silence on the other end. Then she hears, "One moment, please." Someone else picks up the phone. "I would like to order some pig tails," she says again. Dead silence. "I want for six people," my mother said in her Swedish accent. The six people included Dad's musicians and some key staff. She tells the guy on the phone, "And also some neck bones please."

Finally, they tell her they don't have any, but can get what she needs delivered in three days. She also gets some black-eyed peas, collard greens, and rice. She waits three days.

When the pig tails arrive, they don't look so good, but the neck bones looked okay. There was my mother in this little kitchenette with six pots, three burners. After cooking for four hours, she had created her first soul food dishes.

When it came time for the dinner party she'd arranged, everybody sat down. Pop sat at the head

My father told me that my mother was the love of his life. She was a calm and loving presence in his life. They were married in 1960, amid a storm of controversy. In fact, their marriage was illegal in thirty one states.

Dean Martin and Pop visit Frank Sinatra on the set of Sinatra's film *Some Came Running*. The chemistry between these three men both on and off stage was one in a million.

of the table. Being a Harlem boy, he was thinking this is going to be sheer humiliation. So immediately my father announced to his guests—who were all on his payroll—"If you don't eat it, you're fired!"

The crew ate every last drop! To my mother's credit, her soul food creation was not half bad, so I was told, considering it was Lake Tahoe and made by a full-blood Swede.

It was an early March morning and Pop was back resting at his home in a hospital bed upstairs in his master suite. Shirley, Lessie Lee, and I had become skilled bedside nurses. Today we were being given instructions from a home nurse as to how to clean Pop's trachea tube. In case of emergency, the nurse wanted to be sure we knew how to prevent airway obstruction, impaired ventilation, and infection as well as other lethal complications.

I was a germaphobe. I was pregnant. I was due in a month. It wasn't just the sickness of it all, it was reality setting in. Dad's hope of recovery was slim to none. But under no circumstance was my father going to let the fear of death stop us from spending time together. We sat in silence for hours, sometimes just holding hands, sometimes laughing our heads off, sometimes chatting about his nostalgic and heroic past, sometimes just smelling the sweet scent from the eucalyptus trees in his garden oasis. Whatever it was, we cherished every moment.

Lessie Lee announced that Uncle Frank was here. Frank Sinatra, oh my! I knew Pop would be hesitant about his friends visiting him in the state he was. Dad didn't like being seen like this but Frank would never take no for an answer and Dad would never say "no."

Uncle Frank entered and had a few comforting words with my father. You could tell he was destroyed by the impending death of his friend. He climbed down the stairs. I followed him down. Uncle Frank was crying like a little kid. I gave him a big bear hug. "How could my best friend be dying?" he said. I took Uncle Frank outside so Pop couldn't hear. We paced around the circular driveway talking. Satellite press trucks and reporters swarmed outside the guard gate.

I found myself comforting a legend, this tough guy. Uncle Frank saw the tears well up in my face and tried to change the subject. He kept repeating my bachelorette night and how much fun it was. Then he would break down again and say: "Trace Face, oh my God. Smokey's dying. . . ." As Uncle Frank departed, choked up and in tears—the paparazzi shooting at him through his car—we made a pact to think of Pop as he always was throughout our lives, not as he was now.

I assisted my father downstairs and out to the brick patio surrounded by his favorite lush emerald garden. We walked out together hearing the little wheels of his IV grind against the brick. He was wearing his hospital gown.

"Grab the robe!" my father said. Lord really, Pop—like I would forget the hospital gown was open!

Our talks outside became a daily ritual with Popsicle leading the way. Do we talk today or have silence? It was always his choice. My father was determined to foster strong emotional bonds between us now, to show me how much he loved me, share his most intimate life stories with me, and laugh and share a smile or two. I hovered and perched over his words like a hummingbird ready to lap up sweet nectar.

Today we just laughed. They say laughter is the best medicine and laugh we did. We were cracking jokes, bantering back and forth, good belly laughs, clutching our sides till it hurt. I always hit Pop's funny bone in just the right way, making him snort and cackle until he had to beg me to stop.

"Pop, remember when you colored your hair with Kiwi shoe polish! It was running down the sides of your face! I laughed my ass off!"

"I had ten minutes till showtime!" Pop was cracking up.

"But Kiwi shoe polish? Really, Pop!"

"Oh, and you never did anything foolish? Every kid wants a dog, right? I buy you a poodle and what do you do? You give it back to me! Now I got this poodle messing up *my* house!"

"Our gift to you, Pop!" I laughed.

"Charming!" He smiled.

"Listen, Pop, I hate to put a damper on our party, but I got a baby checkup. I'll be back in the morning. Let me get Lessie Lee or the nurse out here," I said.

"Okay, Trace Face, but don't forget I'm ready. I'm gonna learn to change diapers, do bottles, I might even babysit!" Dad said happily.

"Oh God," I said.

"And, Trace, plan to spend the whole day visiting tomorrow, okay?" Pop said, holding his trach hole.

"Sure. Why, Pop, what's up?" I said.

"Gasser, chickie baby, we're going to relive the glory days of the Rat Pack! In honor of Frank. You with me?"

"I'm already packed," I replied with a big grin on my face.

CHAPTER 3

STAR

My father in his prime, one of
the biggest stars of his day

When I arrived the next morning, Pop was in his chaise lounge out in his emerald garden landscape, enjoying the simple pleasures of watching the butterflies flutter from flower to flower. He felt the new spring breeze wash over his face. He cherished the serenity of silence.

I quietly sat down next to him, so as not to disturb his Zen-like state of spiritual healing. But I could feel the pain of the cancer weighing heavily on the life he was no longer living. I wanted to ask him how he felt, but I knew it would hurt him, so I kept my mouth shut and let it hurt me instead. He could feel my angst. He took my hand in his.

"I earned my stripes with those cats. . . ."

"What cats?"

"The Rat Pack . . ."

The ensemble of Frank Sinatra, Dean Martin, Peter Lawford, Joey Bishop, and their closest friends in the late 1950s and '60s was christened the Rat Pack, as a successor of sorts to Humphrey Bogart's 1950s Holmby Hills Rat Pack. Mom said she never liked that name. Actor Tony Curtis said: "We didn't like the term Rat Pack. I hated it, so did Frank, so did Sammy, all of us hated it. Our group of friends was named that by the intelligencia of New York City—the Aryan population of the far right. Here we were all children of immigrants—Hungarian immigrants, Italian immigrants, Russian immigrants, and Sammy being black."

"The price of admission was talent, and most of all love and respect," said Dad. I loved them like brothers. Before I was widely accepted by the world, I was accepted and loved by them. Off the stage, inside our circle, there were no color boundaries. Back in the day, when Frank was singing at the Copa, I was turned away at the door because I was colored. By 1954, the Copacabana ushered me through the door like a big star because I was with Frank Sinatra. He was not just 'the Voice'; to me, he was the voice against racism," Pop said.

"He respected your talent," I uttered.

"We respected each other's talent. I met up with Frank again in 1947 over a sandwich, when I was still just 'the Kid.'"

"I remember him studying Tommy Dorsey's breathing, just to perfect his own voice." Pop was starting to repeat himself, slip a bit, repeat stories he had long since told me, something I noticed, but wouldn't let get in our way.

"A class act," I replied.

"I remember telling Terry Wogan, about how Frank and I reunited. I called it the second beginning of our relationship," Dad said.

"What happened, Pop?"

"I was just out of the army, still wearing my army suit with the gold bird on it. In those days, if you were a discharged soldier, you could get free tickets to shows at NBC, CBS, wherever. So I got tickets to the *Old Gold Show* with Frank Sinatra. I had been in the audience three weeks in a row, and Frank kept looking out at me—the black cat in the audience. Back then, not too many black folks were going to see Frank Sinatra."

"One day, Frank comes out of the stage door and

Dad sure made a lot of close friends over the years of his career. Among them in these photos are James Dean, Frank Sinatra, Nat King Cole, Jerry Lewis, and Richard Burton.

says, 'Didn't we work together?' I told him 'Yes, it was only three days, we replaced an act when you were with Tommy Dorsey.' He remembered! I couldn't believe it!" Pop explained.

"Then Frank said, 'You were with your family?' I nodded. Frank said, 'Hey, you're out of the army, want to come next week?' I said, 'Oh, could I?' I was so excited. 'Yeah, come and watch rehearsal.'"

"Frank turned to his manager, who was Hank Sanicola at the time, 'See Charley over here,' so I broke in and said, 'My name is Sammy.' Frank replied, 'It's Charley. See Charley over here? When he comes here make sure he gets in for the rehearsal.' He turned to me and said, 'See you next week, kid,' got in his car, and drove off," Pop explained.

"That's a great story, Pop." I smiled.

"I was in heaven. After, I walked to the hotel we were living in, from Hollywood down to Fifth Street in Los Angeles. Man, it must have been twenty miles. I just walked like I was in heaven, floating lightly through the streets. I had met Frank Sinatra and he remembered me! It was the second beginning of our relationship," my father said proudly.

"You idolized him." I laughed.

"Heck, I wanted to be like him, I wanted to dress like him, I wanted to look like him, I took my hair and had it all done up, Sinatra style, with the little curl here and all." Dad pointed to his hair.

Dad in performance in the late '50s

"That's sweet, Pop." I said.

"I watched Frank's climb to fame, his fall, his comeback, his obsession with JFK, and through it all he was always the voice. I can see him now, onstage, perched on the bar stool with his brim hat tilted back, jacket languidly tossed over one shoulder, with that smooth sultry voice that made girls scream.

"During the Rat Pack days, Frank and I had a close camaraderie of musicians and entertainers, stage hands—colors and ranks would fade away. It was our home. Never a regret. That's why I called one of my autobiographies, *Why Me?* I always looked to God, during the good times and the bad, and would say, 'Why Me?' Frank was a blessing from God. We got so in sync onstage, all I had to do was raise my eyebrow a certain way and he knew what I was saying. We honed our craft."

The great comedian Milton Berle later said, "Every one of them that were in the Rat Pack was dedicated to their art. I wasn't part of the Rat Pack but I was friends with them all. They were so relaxed. Everything was ad lib. Everything was impromptu. I think that the success of the Rat Pack—besides loving what they did, making people laugh, and truly liking each other—was fun."

My father continued his stories about the Rat Pack. "After the shows at the Sands, baby, we were wild. Innocent compared to today maybe, but we were wild. Hey, we were the headliners, the ladies were the most attractive, the cats the coolest, the booze the best, the celebrities the highest profilers, the ragtag misfits the freakiest. But you learn. Now that I am older, wiser, it's payback time, boy, on my body—for all those good times from the '60s. Years later, every once in a while when I tried to get out of one of those low sports cars, my body said to me, 'I told you to take it easy.' I'd be like ew, ah, ow . . . well, I think I'll just sit here for a while then!" Pop chuckled.

All five core members of the Rat Pack teamed up to star in the movie *Ocean's 11*, which went into production in Las Vegas in January 1960. The original writer of the story, Jack Golden Russell, was a gas-station attendant in Vegas, and handed Sinatra the script while he was filling up. Just like Frank to accept it. There was, of course, a famous remake of *Ocean's 11*, made in 2001 starring George Clooney, Matt Damon, and other hot stars of the day. In the 1960 edition, Danny Ocean (Frank Sinatra) gathers a gang of World War II 82nd Airborne compatriots to pull off the ultimate Las Vegas casinos heist. The plan is to rob five casinos on New Year's Eve (Sahara, Riviera, Desert Inn, Sands, and The Flamingo).

Pop always said, a huge portion of *Ocean's 11* was improvised, ad-libbed. The Rat Pack knew each other and the Vegas casinos better than any screenwriter could ever attempt to write. Much of the Rat Pack ad-libbed dialogue turned out to be far better footage than what they would have shot from the written script, so the producers went with it. Even Shirley MacLaine ad-libbed a tipsy uncredited cameo with a classic Dean Martin line, "I'm so drunk I don't think I could lie down without holding on." I've read that MacLaine received a brand new car from Warner Bros. as compensation for her memorable contribution.

Angie Dickinson was the female lead in the movie. She later said, "Sammy is the one who recommended me for the movie . . . so Sammy told me. And I believe him! I was under contract to Warner Bros. and he said to Frank, 'You know who'd be a gas as your wife? Angie!' I got the part." Frank had a lot of pull in the industry. Angie Dickinson continued to say that "Frank was a very kind man. We think he was all gruff . . . he could throw you out the window and over the balcony if you did something to deserve that, but he was a very tender guy—very!"

Pop played a garbage collector, Josh Howard, in the movie. He said he needed wooden blocks attached to the pedals on the garbage truck he drove in the film so he could reach them. He also said the production team's most challenging task was trying to get Nevada's Clark County officials to lend them a garbage truck for the movie. Needless to say, they finally got the truck. Peter, Dean, and Frank have a scene near the end of the film where they attempt to disguise themselves by blackening their faces in the garbage truck. Pop, as Josh, says, "I knew this color would come in handy someday." Forever more, Uncle Frank and Uncle Dean joked with Pop about that line, all in good fun.

During the filming of *Ocean's 11*, Pop's schedule was insane. The ensemble continued to perform

A movie poster for *Ocean's 11*. Illustrated from left are
Frank Sinatra, Dean Martin, Pop, Peter Lawford, and Angie Dickinson.

TOP: "The Summit": Peter Lawford, Frank Sinatra, Dean Martin, Dad, and Joey Bishop during the time they were making *Ocean's 11*.

BOTTOM: The stars of *Ocean's 11*

RIGHT: The Rat Pack in all their glory.

concurrently at the Sands Hotel each night, in an extravaganza they referred to as "the Summit." I heard it was a reference to the East-West Paris summit that took place that year between the United States, the USSR, United Kingdom, and France.

"The way we did our shows, we made it look like all fun and games. But we worked hard. Like I said, we were wild, but how hard can you really party when you perform one to two shows a night and are due in for call-time and makeup on a major feature film the next morning, sometimes before sunrise? The only time we got any decent sleep was in the afternoons, after the shoot before a show," Pop explained.

I always loved the final shot of *Ocean's 11*, when the eleven compatriots referred to in the title walk past the Rat Pack's own famous marquee in front of the Sands hotel—Frank Sinatra, Dean Martin, Sammy Davis Jr, Peter Lawford, and Joey Bishop. The last billed, Joey Bishop, was also the last of the Rat Pack to pass away, on October 17, 2007.

Dad as Jonah Williams in *Sergeants 3*, 1962

ABOVE: Producer Budd Schulberg visits Dad on the set of a television special, "Memory in White," in 1961.

RIGHT: Dad made an appearance in the 1962 movie *Three Penny Opera*.

Pop approached his rigid schedule like clock-work, never missing a beat. 1961 began a period of Rat Pack activities for Dad that included a whirl-wind of making movies, among them *Sergeants 3*, *Robin and the 7 Hoods*, and *Johnny Cool*.

There were "Summit" performances with Uncle Frank and Uncle Dean in Atlantic City in August 1962. There were shows at the Villa Venice in Chicago in November 1962, and back at the Sands Hotel in both January and September of 1963.

"Frank asked me to work John F. Kennedy's campaign show. He was obsessed with getting JFK elected—pushed favors with the mob to turn West Virginia and Chicago voters in favor of JFK. But really that was none of my business, though, there are rumors to the contrary. I can tell you after working the JFK campaign show, I was delighted that JFK received the Democratic party's presidential ballot in 1960. I wasn't thrilled about Mississippi booing me when I sung the national anthem, though. But no racial slurs surprised me by that point. Brush it off and move on was my motto!" Pop explained.

"What about Joe Kennedy? I heard some stories about him!" I said.

"I got one story about Ambassador Kennedy I bet you have never heard."

"What happened?" I asked.

"Awww, well, poor Peter Lawford was just a kid, sixteen years old, parking cars on the wrong side of town in West Palm Beach, Florida, for twenty-five bucks a week. Peter became buddies with two black valet cats he worked with. One day, a rich client saw Peter on break, eating lunch and playing cards with his colored buddies. The rich client was outraged and complained to the parking lot owner that it was a disgrace to see such a good-looking white boy frat-ernizing with colored kids. Poor Peter almost lost his job. Turns out the client was Joe Kennedy. How Peter survived being Joe Kennedy's son-in-law fif-teen years later is beyond me!" Pop said.

"How did you survive being the son-in-law to mom's father? I mean he was Swedish, she was

Dad in the 1962 film *Convicts 4*

Swedish, interracial marriages were forbidden by law in thirty-one states when you got married." I asked.

"I adored my father-in-law, and your mother said he loved me, too. Your grandparents didn't have an ounce of racism in them. They were kind, loving, and supportive. Incredible folks. That's why your mother was the way she was," Pop smiled.

"I remember my first appearance as an enter-

tainer in London. I was booked for a $12,000-a-week nightclub act at the Pigalle in London. Your mom was already telling friends she'd probably become Mrs. D, but she was finalizing her divorce from [Edwin] Eddie Gregson, son of a distinguished widower and Southern California real estate millionaire. Your mom flew to London to see my show, and flew her father in from Sweden. She was determined to introduce her own father to her 'soon-to-be groom,'" Pop said.

"That's so sweet. . . ."

"Luckily, her father had already gone back to our London hotel and didn't have to see the hate banners and all the public booing outside the Pigalle. Your mom and I had to face horrible insults from bigots. About thirty followers of Sir Oswald Mosley waved banners saying, 'Go home, Nigger' and 'Get divorced first, Slag' in reference to my plans to marry your mom after her divorce was final," Pop explained.

"As I always say, being a star made it possible for me to get insulted in places where the average Negro could never hope to get insulted!" Pop smirked.

"Gosh, and you two were only just dating," I replied.

"Your mom was like Grace Kelly with all the elegance, beauty, class, and charm, but fierce as a tiger. She told the London press that her love for me could not be destroyed by fascist hate attacks," Pop explained.

"A kind British journalist for the *Daily Mirror*, by

the name of Sir William Neil Connor came to our defense, pleading for people to stop the slander, get off our backs, enough was enough." The guy wrote under the pen name of "Cassandra" taken from Greek mythology, in reference to a tragic character given the gift of prophecy by Apollo but is ultimately cursed so that no one will believe her.

"Your mom continued to pay the price for the London racial slurs, though. Back in Hollywood, eighteen days after the racial slurs by Sir Oswald Mosley's followers in London, a Twentieth Century-Fox spokesman released a statement that May Britt's contract would not be renewed," Pop explained. "This was June 1960. The studio refused to say if the action was a result of her plans to marry me or the London racial slurs, but the timing was more than a coincidence."

I could see my father's eyelids grow heavier. Mentally, our talks were therapeutic for both of us, but physically draining for him. I put a throw blanket over him and let him nod off for a spell. As I watched him sleep, I thought of my mom, always so

With Henry Silva in *Johnny Cool*, 1963

Uncle Frank, Dad, and Uncle Dean
in *Robin and the 7 Hoods*, 1964

proper on the outside, dressed to perfection, bag hanging on her forearm, never leaving the house without her eyeliner—she was so put together, so beautiful. On the inside, she had enormous courage, strength, and resilience. She would not only marry a black man at a time when interracial marriages were shunned, but do it at all costs.

My mom, Swedish actress May Britt Wilkens was born on March 22, 1934, in Lidingö, Sweden. Her birth name was MajBritt Wilkens, but she later changed it to May Britt. Her father, Hugo Brigg-Wilkens, was a postal clerk; her mother, a housewife. Mom had a younger sister named Margot. Mom always said there was very little racism in Sweden, at least in the town where she grew up.

Mom and Dad had a deep, undying love for each other, while courting, through marriage, and divorce—even after my father's death.

Mom always said, "It was your father's kindness, his thoughtfulness that interested me the most. He was very intelligent. He studied people, he understood people—he could always spot someone across the room and tell if they were a phony or not."

Mom still says, "He was a good father, Trace, even if his schedule kept him from being around all the time. As an entertainer, when you are hot you are hot, you have to work. Can't stay home and hold your wife's hand all the time. Your father had to work his butt off. And it was also his life blood, his passion. He thrived on it. He loved entertaining."

Mom had a great career before she met my father. Her first job was as a photographer's laboratory assistant in the Stockholm suburb where she was born. At eighteen years old, she left for Italy. In 1952, she was discovered by producer Carlo Ponti at a retouching studio. My mother became one of fifty actresses who Ponti auditioned for the film *Yolanda, Daughter of the Black Pirate*. Mom landed the role and off to Rome she went, chaperoned by her own mother, for the filming of *Yolanda*. In 1957, my mother moved to the United States after five years under contract to Carlo Ponti in Italy.

In 1957, Mom escorted her good friend, Montgomery Clift, to the Hollywood premiere of the American Civil War drama *Raintree Country*, a film in which he starred with Elizabeth Taylor. Clift had a nearly fatal car accident during the filming, which is evident in scenes where the left side of his face was partially paralyzed. The director of *Raintree Country*, Edward Dmytryk, would later direct my mom in the 1959 film *The Blue Angel*. Mom fit in well in Hollywood. She and fellow Swedish starlet Ingrid Goude were invited to the filming of television's *Panorama Pacific*. Mom was also cast in the role of Kristina "Kris" Abbott in *The Hunters*—a Twentieth Century-Fox feature film adapted from a novel by James Salter.

In 1958, Mom attended a dinner party given by Southern California real-estate mogul Edwin Gregson Sr. My mother met his son, Eddie Gregson. Eddie

Taken on the day my parents announced their engagement to the world, 1960

BELOW: My mother and grandmother, Elvera Sanchez

RIGHT: Mom and Marilyn Monroe, as houseguests of Frank Sinatra. Mom was pregnant with me at the time.

left Stanford University in 1957 to follow an acting career, getting a small part in *The Naked and the Dead*. My mother spent a lot of time with young Gregson on the Strip and in Malibu, and on February 22, 1958, Mom and Eddie Gregson married in Tijuana, Mexico. He was nineteen; she was twenty-three.

Although Mom and Eddie found a nice house in which to live way up in the Canyon, Mom's relationship with the young Gregson was not destined to rise much higher. The two parted for the first time when she returned to Sweden alone and he was off on a movie assignment. In June 1958, Mom returned to the States, followed by my aunt Margot. Mom and Eddie reunited in a new house in Palo Alto. Gregson left the film business, with dreams of returning to Stanford to study law. By late October, Mom was sent to New York City to do publicity for *The Hunters*. There she took photography courses, while Eddie went to San Antonio, Texas, to serve with the Air National Guard for two months.

Mom became an overnight sensation on film posters and magazine covers galore after she won

My mom all in white, Dad all in black. Pop courted controversy while courting my mother,
but they didn't care—they were in love!

the part in *The Blue Angel*. The film was a remake of the 1930 classic of the same name that had made Marlene Dietrich a star. The part had previously been slated for no less a star than Marilyn Monroe. Mom said there was never any tension between her and Marilyn. She said, "Years later we were house-guests at Sinatra's place. Marilyn, like me, was shy. Neither of us were the life of the party. I was pregnant with you at the time, and Marilyn and I had our picture taken together. Later it became quite a famous shot."

In the summer of 1959, Mom planned a trip to Sweden to visit her parents with her husband. Eddie announced his plans to take summer classes at Stanford. Tension mounted. Mom asked her husband not to visit the set when she was singing for *The Blue Angel*. Mom and Eddie soon announced their separation. With her marriage unraveling, Mom turned down a role in the film *The Seven Thieves*, a part that went to Joan Collins instead.

Mom had become quite well known. Her marriage was on the rocks and the press was on it. Mom was feisty when it came to the press. In March 1960, she told columnist Earl Carroll at the Sherry-Netherland Hotel in New York City: "My name is My! I hate to be called May!" Columnist Dorothy Kilgallen reported in August 1959: "May Britt's split with her husband, Ed Gregson, wasn't much of a surprise to local cafe-goers . . ." By September 8, 1959, Mom and Eddie separated for good. Mom filed for divorce two days later in Santa Monica, ending her nineteen-month marriage. By the end of

September, Mom had an interlocutory divorce decree from Gregson. But the divorce was yet to be finalized.

Mom next filmed *Murder, Inc.* at Filmways Studio in New York City. She was expected to return to Hollywood and then on to Hawaii to board and surf at Waikiki. But instead my dad entered the picture and changed her life forever.

My mother attended one of Pop's shows at the Mocambo nightclub, which opened in 1941 at the site of the old Club Versailles on the Sunset Strip in Los Angeles. "Your father was in a car with a female friend. He saw me walk across the street, and told his friend he wanted to meet me," Mom still recalled about fifty years later. "He called me, told me after the show a group of people would be going up to his house on Evanview Drive above the Sunset Plaza to watch a movie, would I care to join?"

"I did join, but what I thought was so endearing, so kind, was that your father drove me all the way home to Malibu after the party. He invited me *and* my mom in town from Sweden to his show at the Sands. I thought that was so nice and thoughtful," Mom explained, smitten.

"I always adored Frank, too," Mom would say. "I remember one time when I was planning on heading to Vegas for one of your father's shows. I had a horrible cold, and told your father I didn't want to come up and get the whole Rat Pack sick. Your father told Frank, 'May's not coming up. She has a cold, doesn't want to make us sick,' and Frank said, 'What a classy broad.'"

Pop had been involved with a twenty-one-year-old Canadian singer named Joan Stewart. He quickly broke things off and began his pursuit of my mom. He even asked his Mama (his grandmother) what she thought about him marrying my mom. Dad had a talk with her. "I'm going to marry May, Mama." Mama liked my mother, but looked at him with the concerned eyes of a wise old woman from Harlem, "I won't say, do you know what's ahead of you, Sammy?"

In April 1960 in New York City, Mom declined to confirm or deny reports to the press that she and Sammy Davis, Jr. were planning to get married—since she was still not officially divorced from Eddie Gregson. Eddie had already moved on and was being seen around town with actress Cara Williams. The Hollywood wedding was scheduled for October 16, 1960, but had to be postponed until November 13 due to technicalities involving my mom's divorce. Finally, on September 28, 1960, Mom's divorce from Gregson became final.

Mom decided to convert to Judaism before her wedding to my father and on October 17, 1960, a spokesman for Hollywood's Temple Israel announced that she was accepted into the faith of Judaism. My father always joked with me about her conversion. As the story goes, he was driving with my mother and she blurted out:

"Sammy, how come you never asked me to convert? To become Yewish?"

My father laughed and said, "Well, for openers, if you keep giving it that Swedish *J*—I don't think

they'd even take you."

My mother smiled, and whipped out her certificate of conversion from Temple Israel. She explained how she was satisfied as a Lutheran, but thought it would add unity and support to the family, once they married and had children, if both parents were of the same religion. Now they could be married by a rabbi.

"Darling, there's no nicer present you could have ever given me," my father said.

Mom replied, "Then you wanted me to convert? Why didn't you say so?"

"I didn't feel I had the right to. I wanted you to do it, only if it was your own desire. I'm the last person in the world to say, 'Do it my way because my way is better,'" Dad said. My father took her hand and kissed it. "Thank you."

Only eight days later, three youths wearing swastika arm bands paraded outside the Huntington Hartford Theater where my father was headlining. Officers had to take my parents into protective custody. But that did not stop them. On November 9, 1960, Mom and Pop took out their marriage license in Los Angeles.

My father postponed the wedding yet again due to the racial tension in the air, the press, and Sinatra's allegiance to JFK. Frank was planning to be his best man, and Dad didn't want him to suffer in the press for it. He just couldn't believe his friendship with Frank could affect a national election, but for JFK, every vote counted, from the liberals to the bigots. Pop had told me that he received a letter one day that read: "Dear Nigger Bastard, I see Frank Sinatra is going to be the best man at your abortion. Well, it's good to know the kind of people supporting Kennedy before it's too late."—An ex-Kennedy Vote

Mom said, "We got death threat letters all the time, but we didn't save them. We just hired a body-guard. It just became a way of life. We heard it so often, we shrugged it off; otherwise we would go crazy. Your father had met JFK several times, was fond of him. He asked me if I would mind putting off the wedding until after the election. It was disappointing, but I was prepared for anything. I knew what I was getting into."

Ostensibly trivial incidents would escalate into major threats and even hate group demonstrations outside places where my father was entertaining. Outside the Lotus Club in Washington, D.C., white picketers carried signs: MARRIAGE TO MAY BRITT WILL BE AN INJUSTICE TO THE NEGRO RACE! and GO BACK TO THE CONGO, YOU KOSHER COON! To my father's credit, when he walked onstage that night, the audience rose to their feet, applauded his courage, and exclaimed, "To hell with 'em, Sammy. We're with you!"

Despite the support from my father's fans, family, and close friends, my mother's parents were forced to send a telegram to all the guests invited to the wedding:

The wedding of Miss May Britt Wilkens and Mr. Sammy Davis, Jr. will be postponed until Sunday, November 13. We sincerely hope your attendance will be possible for the wedding reception at the Beverly Hilton Hotel on this day at 4:00 p.m. RSVP 9057 Dicks Street, Los Angeles 46, California.

—Mr. and Mrs. Ernst Hugo Wilkens

My parents on their wedding day, 1960

The thoughts of my parents' unyielding love was disrupted by a nurse who came outside to check on my father. He woke up as she tried to quietly adjust his IV and trachea tube. Lessie Lee had already placed some beverages and snacks on the table by his chaise lounge.

"Hey, Trace Face, you get uglier every time I see you." His eyes sparkled with joy as if I had just entered.

"How are feeling, Pop?" I asked.

"How are *you* feeling is the question, Ms. Pregasaurus?" Pop said.

"I'm fine. Sam's kicking a bit."

"Learning how to kick butt early, that's my grandson!" Pop replied, holding his trach hole to speak.

I thought about how exciting it was that here I am, married and having my first child. I recalled a story my father had told me about his wedding to my mother.

First of all, since my father had to postpone the wedding for almost a month, thanks to death threats, demonstrations, and JFK's election, by the time they got married, my mother was already pregnant with me.

My parents wanted a dignified wedding, not a publicity circus about this taboo interracial marriage. So they had a small, private ceremony at their Hollywood home on Evanview Drive off the Sunset Strip. The reception was at the Beverly Hilton Hotel with around two hundred guests. Some of the press claimed my mother was twenty-four but she was really twenty-six. My father was thirty-four. Since my mother had already converted to Judaism the Jewish rites were performed by Rabbi William Kramer of Hollywood's Temple Israel. It was beautiful, so I heard.

Frank stood up with my father. Mama, my Grandfather, Uncle Will, my grandparents from Sweden, were there, among others. The guests watched on in the living room with a canopy of flowers by the windows—under which stood my parents as bride and groom. Shirley was the maid of honor.

Pop was so deeply in love with my mother. His whole life, he said he felt alone, in the army and all. Once he met my mother, he didn't feel alone anymore. She was the love of his life—his joy, his better half. When Mom appeared from the next room with her father, looking like a Swedish goddess in her dress, tears welled up in my father's eyes. He was a superstar, but she was an icon, at least to him.

The words of Rabbi William Kramer are words that should never be forgotten—ever. They should live on forever.

This is what he said to my parents:

"*Almighty God, supremely blessed, supreme in might and glory, guide and bless this groom and his bride. Sammy and May, you are standing in front of me to join your lives even as your hands are joined together, and custom dictates that I, as your rabbi, give you some advice.*

"*Your marriage is something more than just the marriage of two people in love, and it is most certainly that or I have never seen two people in love in twenty years of the ministry. But as you come together as man and wife something more is involved. You are people without prejudice. You represent the value of the society that many of us dream about but, I suspect, hesitate to enter. As such, because you are normal in an abnormal society—society will treat you as sick. To be healthy among the sick is to be treated as sick as if the others were healthy.*

"*Through no fault of your own except your love, because both of you are greater than the pettiness that divide men, you become not simply a symbol of marriage, but because you both have accepted Judaism equally as your own you become representatives of Judaism because you are in the public eye; you are part of that from which the public gets its response and its value systems—either by acting along with or reacting to.*

"*Also, because of the circumstances of your love, there is a symbolic representation to the fact that you are of different racial stocks originally and that now you merge your love as in a sense all mankind is merging its genes and chromosomes to the oneness which is inevitable. It's not really fair that your love should have so much imposed upon it, but it must be a mark of greatness of your love to know that you must not only continue to love each other, but because circumstances beyond control—and all circumstances involved in real love are beyond control—make you representatives of Judaism and marriage to a world that watches with curiosity, with eagerness, almost with a will to see failure rather than success.*

"*An additional pressure is on you in knowing that because of the different racial backgrounds you are a symbol, too, of the success that must come from such unions. If you are true to the story of your love, then your social role in our times will be an important one. Important for the future of the amity of races.*

"*What I pray for you, May, and for you, Sammy, is the strength that you may fulfill either the public role or private role, because if you can do either, you will be doing both. If you are true to that which you have called upon yourselves or which has been thrust upon you by society, then your love will be a love story to join immortal love stories of the ages.*

"*May the blessings of the patriarchs and the prophets, may the blessings of God Almighty be upon you and may you be worthy, my dear friends, of a historic trust and a great love.*"

Mom and Dad's marriage was so controversial they required bodyguards.

After that Rabbi Kramer led them into their "I do's." I turned to my father, who was smiling.

"Thank you Trace Face. That lifted my spirits. It energizes me to think of the good ole days. Your mom was glowing in every wedding photo."

"She was glowing all right! Glowing with a one hundred three degree fever," I said.

"It's true. Your mother was so sick. She was in bed before the ceremony and after!" Pop exclaimed.

"Mom said the doctor told her she had an intestinal flu and had to stay in bed."

"And your mother told the doctor: 'You're crazy! It's my wedding!'"

"Mom always told me, 'your poor father had to go to the reception by himself, without his bride!'"

"What she said to me after the reception, in her Swedish decoding process was, 'Poor Sharlie Brown had to go alone to his own wedding party!'"

"Sharlie Brown, that's funny. You were Charlie Brown, too. A solo groom at the Beverly Hilton Hotel with no bride and swarms of guests to entertain!" Among the guests were Peter Lawford and his wife, Diana Dors, Tony Curtis, Barbara Rush, Jack Kelly, Mr. and Mrs. Dean Martin, Peter Brown, Janet Leigh, Shirley MacLaine, Edward Robinson Jr., Milton Berle, the list goes on and on.

The public outrage after the wedding was so vitriolic, my parents were forced to hire bodyguards—again! More frenzied hate letters, more death threats. Uncle Frank was hosting Kennedy's inaugural party. Pop even got removed from the list of entertainers. He was deeply hurt by that. In her column, journalist Dorothy Kilgallen wrote at the time, "Scuttlebutt from the Clan indicates Frank Sinatra and chums will take over a whole floor of Washington's best hotels for the inauguration ceremonies in January. Big question: Since the nation's capital isn't very integrated will Sammy Davis, Jr., be allowed to share a suite with his bride, May Britt?"

I started to think about my own interracial wedding decades later. My husband, Guy Garner, was Italian; I am mixed, so the potential for future hardship ran through my father's mind. Dad used to talk about his love for Guy. He gave us his wisdom about interracial marriage: "Just remember, it's their problem, not yours."

When I got married, Pop and I had just overcome obstacles in our father-daughter relationship—my father had been too busy to attend childhood birthday parties, my college graduation, and such. To make up for the past, my father was determined to do everything right at my wedding. He watched *Father of the Bride* like he was studying for a role, to prepare for my wedding. It was sweet, and he nailed it.

I remember when my husband and I were at Pop's private pool at the Desert Inn one time in Vegas. We decide to head to the main pool to swim. Dad stopped us and screamed, "No!!!!!" Then he caught himself and said, "Sorry, kids, I forgot we're not in the '60s anymore . . . go on, have fun!"

I glanced over at Pop in his chaise lounge. His head was down. I guessed he was still thinking about not being invited to the JFK inaugural party. I tried to cheer him up, "So not long after your wedding to Mom, I was born! Tee hee!"

"July 5, 1961. Best day of my life after marrying your mom!" Pop perked up.

"Mom said she went to the bathroom and realized her water broke," I said.

"A couple of weeks early at that! We jumped in the car along with our close friends, the Boyars. Anyway, I drove to the hospital, and your mom sat next to me in the passenger seat—moaning."

"Mom said in the car on the way to the hospital, you heard on the radio that you were on the way to the hospital!" I said.

"Yeah, isn't that a kick? We all got a good laugh out of that one!" Pop chuckled. "Once we got to Cedars, your mom was given a spinal. In those days the fathers had to wait in the waiting room, so that's what I did."

"Mom says if you had been in the operating room, you would have fainted!" I said.

"Your mom couldn't be more correct!" Pop smiled.

"But when I first laid eyes on you in the private room, I got so teary eyed, I just couldn't believe how beautiful you were," Pop said.

"Mom said, all you kept saying was, 'she's so beautiful, she's so beautiful . . .'" I replied.

LEFT: My parents agreed to postpone their wedding at the behest of Frank Sinatra, because they thought it might hurt JFK's run for the presidency. By the time they were wed, my mother was already pregnant with me. I was born July 5, 1961, eight months after their marriage.

ABOVE AND RIGHT: Family photos with Mom, Dad, and my brother Mark, 1962

"Correct again! But your beauty faded quick when you were a toddler, Trace Face," Pop joked. "You liked to pee on me when you were pissed!"

"But . . . for three days in that hospital, your mother and I were so touched, so moved by you, our first child, our only daughter, Tracey Hillivi Davis." [Hillivi was my Swedish grandmother's first name.]

"When we left the hospital, press was swarming everywhere. They kept asking 'What color is the baby?'" Pop said.

"I heard they asked, 'What color is IT?'" I chimed in.

"Even worse!" Pop exclaimed. "We climbed into our Rolls Royce and took off, thrilled to leave the press behind. You know, Trace, I never used to let those type of comments get to me. Even when my own people would complain to me about racism, I would always say, 'You got it easy. I'm a short, ugly, one-eyed, black Jew. What do you think it's like for me?'"

The nurse came out to give my dad some medication and check on him. Pop motioned her away, so we could continue our talk. He was enjoying our moment. He was having a good day, feeling better.

"Your mother and I spoke about adopting kids way back when we were dating. We both believed in providing a good home for children in need. In

My parents on the steps of the courthouse after adopting my brother Jeff, 1965

November 1962, we adopted your brother, two-and-a-half-year-old Mark. A couple of years later, we adopted your brother Jeff. He was four months old. What joy they brought to our lives. What a kick to watch your white Swedish mom carting around three black children!" Pop said.

"The rainbow tribe," I replied.

"As I recall, only you got to meet your grandparents in Sweden before they passed away. Your mother took Jeff to Sweden but only to visit her sister. Her parents were already gone."

"Did you go on the Sweden trips, too?" I asked.

"Trace Face, I was working; my schedule was crazy hectic. First of all, even before you were born, I was juggling films in Hollywood, shows in Vegas, the Rat Pack gigs, *and* making albums! 1957 to 1960 was probably my busiest time with Decca Records, *ever.* I made a swinging album with the Count Basie Band, two duet albums with Carmen McRae, worked with Mundell Lowe, had arrangements by Buddy Bregman. Rigid schedule."

"Sounds like a good gig with Decca Records, though. Why did you leave?" I asked.

"Uncle Frank. He created his own record label, Reprise Records. I left Decca; he left Capitol. Uncle Frank even got Count Basie, Duke Ellington, Bing Crosby, and Dean Martin to sign on his label. Uncle Frank looked out for artists' rights, so we all felt safe. In our contracts, if you chose, recorded masters would become the property of the artist after a period of time, or you could cash out. Either way, Frank looked after us, took care of us. There was

trust," Pop said.

"Trust is everything in the biz," I replied.

"Trust is everything in life. That's why I chose Marty Paich. I trusted his work with my buddy Mel Tormé at Bethlehem and Verve. Paich had this West Coast jazz–style approach to music. Together we made some of the best recordings of my career: *The Wham of Sam* and my hit single 'What Kind of Fool Am I?,' which was on the 1962 *Billboard* charts for fifteen weeks . . ."

"And won the Grammy for Record of the Year!" I added.

My father's musical recording career from 1961 to 1964 was at its height. He had Broadway show-stopper albums, a collaboration with Sam Butera and the Witnesses, a live album recorded at the Cocoanut Grove, an album of songs composed by Mel Tormé, one with Count Basie, and even the cast recording from his second Broadway musical, *Golden Boy.* In 1965, Pop became a Tony Award nominee for Best Actor in a Musical for *Golden Boy.*

"My schedule was tight, but I did my best to make time for your mom, too," Pop said. "We went to the rainy Hollywood premiere of *West Side Story* in December 1961. Not long after, at a New York nightclub, your mom impressed the crowds by dancing the Twist. She impressed me, too, since your mom had no rhythm at all."

"You go, Mom! And don't forget the Funky Chicken."

"Oh," Pop said. "let's not do that . . ."

"Never forget that April, [columnist] Hedda

Jeff Nathaniel Davis, my parents' second adoptive son. I nicknamed him "Bumba."

Hopper came up to me at the Sands and asked if me and your mom were separating. Can you imagine? She heard a rumor, she said. I told her, 'Nothing could be further from the truth. I'm closing here and the next day we leave for Seattle for our first honeymoon,'" Pop said.

"In May, we even took a week off for a vacation in Rome where I was working. Your mother mispronounced almost everything in English. But I found it endearing. I called it the decoding process—one of the reasons I loved her so."

"But oddly enough, when it came to other foreign languages, she could translate anything. In Rome, she translated the Italian so well. I could never have gotten by without her. I remember joking with your mother, that she spoke so many languages it was funny English wasn't one of them." Pop smiled.

"I really didn't like to travel without her to foreign countries, but when I did, I would always bring her back fabulous gifts. One time I was in Paris, I spent a fortune on some French couture Balmain dresses, coats—everything hand-sewn. Beautiful! When your mom found out how much it cost just to get the stuff out of Customs she almost cried!" Pop laughed.

"Don't make me laugh!" I was chuckling.

"When you mother could join me in my travels, Lessie Lee took care of you kids like you were her own. She raised you children like my Mama raised me, over-protective!"

"My Mama loved to tell this story: When I was an infant she would stroll me down the streets of Harlem. When the other mothers would see her coming, they would exclaim, 'Here comes Rosa B with her Jesus!'"

"At least Mama didn't smother you in vats of Vaseline like Lessie Lee did to us!" I told Pop.

"Where's the vat!" My father shouted toward the kitchen, "Lessie Lee! Get the vat out, my daughter's got ashy black feet!" Pop said. In an instant, Lessie Lee marched outside with her vat of Vaseline. We all laughed.

"Lessie Lee, do you remember smothering so much Vaseline on my face, I could barely see?" I ask.

"Uh-huh." Lessie Lee's standard response.

"My vision was so blurred, I couldn't see my way back to the bed for ten minutes! No amount of blinking would get rid of that, it was like a coat on my eyeballs!"

"Uh-huh." Lessie Lee said again, and took the vat back into the house.

"I love Lessie Lee's strong-soulful-black-woman 'Uh-huh'—letting you know she's been around the

My parents adopted my brother Mark in 1963, when he was almost three years old.

My parents in 1966

block a few times. No explanation needed!" I said.

"I got that 'Uh-huh' from Lessie Lee when I told her that your mother and I were going to meet Martin Luther King for the first time. We attended a mass civil rights rally at Wrigley Field in Los Angeles. Lessie Lee's 'Uh-huh' translated to: it's about time you and Dr. King meet, no explanation needed!" Pop said.

In 1963 my father marched with Dr. King at the March on Washington. He campaigned relentlessly against segregation. By the time he was a superstar, Pop forced clubs and casinos across the country to integrate. Back in the day the only place colored folks could hang out in Vegas was the Moulin Rouge.

Burt Boyar was a life-long friend who wrote about my father and the March on Washington in detail. This is what he recounted:

"I was privileged to meet Sammy Davis, Jr. in the mid-1950s and had a friendship that deepened over

On his 1961 trip to London Pop was presented to the Queen Mother at a
Royal Command Performance. He was overwhelmed by the honor.

the years until his death in 1990. Over the course of that friendship, Sammy and I conducted many conversations that were recorded and used for his autobiographies *Yes, I Can* and *Why Me?* But in neither of those books did we touch on his role in the Civil Rights Movement or his thoughts on August 28, 1963. I have since shared this story in a book of photos taken by Sammy throughout his life, *Photo by Sammy Davis, Jr.* Below, in his own words, are Sammy's recollection of that momentous day:

"We left early, first thing, flying out of Detroit to Washington. We got in and it was early in the morning and it was already happening. The streets were alive and buzzing. . . .

"I was scared. You know, wonder what's going to happen? The anticipation of what was going to

TOP RIGHT: The 1963 Civil Rights March on Washington. Pop is being interviewed with Roy Wilkins, executive secretary of the NAACP.

BOTTOM RIGHT: Writer James Baldwin, my father, and Martin Luther King, Jr.

BELOW: With Martin Luther King outside of Pop's dressing room at the Majestic Theater in New York, 1965

happen. They were saying things like, if ten thousand people show up it'll be something. You know, maybe twenty thousand at best. And all the police! Within around three hours of arriving, you knew there was not going to be a riot. Everybody was smiling. And the malcontents were kept so far away that they couldn't interfere. You saw everybody, you saw them all. Lerone Bennett and a few other of the guys from Johnson Publications, *Ebony*, and *Jet*, a few of the photographers, black and white photographers that I knew. We were standing on the steps before the speakers started. Then King got there. And I'm standing, looking down from Lincoln down to the Washington Monument, and going, it's going to be a good day, man, and everybody started smiling and you knew there ain't going to be no trouble. This is going to be great. This is what we prayed for. And it was like a virus that spread among the people. It was everybody. I saw little vignettes of things. People touching, holding hands, probably black people who had never touched white people, or hugged or had a physical line of communication before in their lives. And vice versa. White people who had never been next to a poor, humble black woman and her child that she's holding and everybody had love, it was unbelievable. It really was an unbelievable day, and I remember somebody saying to me, come on, sit on the podium. And I said, no—I can't see from the podium. I want to see

Dad in 1962, in his prime, putting on someone else's records at a press luncheon.

it. I want to be out front. And one of the guys from *Ebony* said, well, Sam, come sit down here. And I went down like in the first, second row, because I was taking pictures and I wanted to be where I could see what was happening, as opposed to being up there looking out at the people. And then afterwards I came up and there were some pictures taken and I walked up to Martin, and everybody was crying, and I just remember saying, thank you. Thank you. And I couldn't say any more than that. And he grabbed me and hugged me and I hugged him, and they swept him away.

"It was a monumental day in many respects. First of all, more than any single incident, the galvanizing of what the Civil Rights Movement was about was that day. It showed that we could live together, the black and whites and Hispanics and everybody else, that we should be pulling together.

"I think it was the most American day in the history of our country, save for perhaps the Battle of Bunker Hill. Or, maybe the signing of the Declaration of Independence. It's to be put on that level, for me, it's on the level of that kind of an occasion.

Twenty years later to the day of the march we all went back. And we recaptured it, the affection, and to see people who had been there twenty years earlier and to see the people who now were there, the young faces, it was joyous. A couple of kids came up to me and said, Sam? You were here before. Is this what it was like? I said: Yeah. Keep it going, man, keep it going.

My father and Peter Lawford in the 1968 film *Salt & Pepper*

My father was feeling in good spirits. "Okay, I got a good Lessie Lee story. I remember after your mom and I got divorced—we'll save that for another day—your mother eventually moved the family to Lake Tahoe. I would do a Harrah's show and ride my three-wheel chopper over to visit with you kids. Your mother would say all excited, 'Oh look, here comes your father on a motorcycle!' and Lessie Lee would mutter under her breath, 'Fool!'" My father laughed hard.

"Lessie Lee is just a character. Mom always said she knew from the first minute she met Lessie Lee that she was the one to help with the kids and stay with our family for a lifetime," I said.

In June 1963, Pop was in Vegas working. Lessie Lee was caring for me and my brother Mark. My mother went off to attend the premiere of *Cleopatra*. She was part of the fourth night charity event or something. There was my mother in the audience, watching the film, when someone tapped her on the shoulder and said, "Your house has been robbed."

"Oh my God, really?" Mom exclaimed.

As the story goes, three men posed as policemen and forced their way into our home on Evanview Drive. The doorbell rang, Lessie Lee looked through the peephole, saw police officers, and opened up the door. They tied up Lessie Lee, took a $15,000 diamond necklace, loads of other jewelry, and at least seven jeweled watches. Thank God, me and Mark were safe, being so young. Lessie Lee was scared out of her mind, poor thing.

"Pop, remember the robbery on Evanview? Is that why you moved to David O. Selznick's mansion in Beverly Hills?" I asked my father.

"Well, we were planning to move, anyway. Your mother was looking for another house. It didn't happen right away, because I remember late that year after the robbery we entertained Bing Crosby and his wife, the actress Kathryn Grant, for dinner and a film in our screening room. We called the screening room 'the playhouse' on Evanview Drive. But one day I was out of town working, and your mother called and said, 'I found this house, it is simply elegant, pure class, doesn't scream gaudy, just breathtaking and homey.' So I told your mother, 'Get it!'" Pop said.

"Sight unseen?" I asked my dad.

"Sight unseen!" Pop said.

"Geez, Pop, you were generous!" I said.

"It cost a fortune back in the day, but happy wife, happy life," Pop said.

My father would not be the only celebrity to own producer David O. Selznick's former mansion over the decades. Ed McMahon and George Hamilton are among the house's other former owners. In 2010, it went on the market at $15.9 million.

The 1934 mansion was designed by Roland Coate and built in Beverly Hills for Selznick, who won a Best

With Cicely Tyson in the 1966 movie *A Man Called Adam*

Judy Garland appeared on Dad's show in 1966 and they performed a memorable musical routine dressed as hobos, just as she had done with Fred Astaire in the film *Easter Parade*.

Picture Oscar for *Gone With the Wind*. It was a simple, traditional house, with all the trimmings of sheer elegance. The house had seven bedrooms and nine bathrooms with more than three-quarters of an acre of manicured grounds including a pool. It had a two-story entry, a formal living room, and a dining room with multiple fireplaces with original Greek keystone-shaped marble. The house had a walk-in bar in the family room, a library, a billiards room, an office, and two maids' quarters.

The nurse came out to check on my father. She suggested that it might be time for Pop to go inside and rest. Together we assisted father inside and up to his bedroom. I gave Pop a kiss on the forehead.

"I had fun today, Popsicle," I told my father.

"Me, too, Trace Face." Pop grinned.

"See you tomorrow. Get some rest. I love you," I said.

"I love you more, baby. Bring me brownies." Pop smiled, then his eyes widened as a new memory came to mind.

"Brownies. Sit down for a sec, I got a story I want to share before you take off," Pop chuckled, "A laced brownie story."

"This ought to be good. . . ." I sat back down.

"Well, you know how focused I was onstage. Something would happen when I walked on stage, there was that magic line, and *poof* that focus was there. Except one time. Someone had sent me some brownies and I didn't know they had put something in them."

"I was munching on these brownies about a half hour before I had to get onstage. And I'm getting stoned. Totally wasted. So Murphy Bennett or Shirley Rhodes, someone comes in and says, 'what are you eating?' I'm like, 'uhmm, these are good, real good,' licking my lips. They took one of the brownies, cracked it in half, and saw a marijuana stem sticking out of it. I hear, 'You got pot in here, someone cooked—oh, get this crap out of here!' I thought, no wonder I am feeling funny."

"Oh, Pop, that's classic!" I said laughing.

"I can hear the guy backstage saying, 'You're on in fifteen, Sammy!' I said, 'What can I do to come down?' Someone in the room said, 'Why don't you drink some hot soup?' Good idea, I think. I love soup, right? They get me some tomato soup, and I drink it out of this big mug. The thing I didn't know is that if you eat marijuana and you drink hot soup, you go through the ceiling. Now by the time the guy announces, 'On in five,' I'm flying high as a kite: 'Yeah baby! I'll be there! Don't worry about it! I'll be there! I'm gonna be there!'"

"Funny!" I'm cracking up now.

"I walked on the stage. I did the opening number, a second number, and I turned to the audience and said, 'I know I have been on a long time, so may I say good night.' I walked off the stage, thinking I had done an hour and twenty minutes. Not. And the audience at the O'Keith Center in Toronto, well, let's just say, I never played back there again." Pop laughed.

"Don't eat what fans send you, Pop," I said, chuckling.

"No joke. Okay, now get your pregnant butt out of here! Love ya, baby!"

"Love ya, too!" And off I went, hollering behind me, "See you for breakfast, I'll bring the brownies!"

In my car on the way home, I thought about the Rat Pack. I remembered a story my father told me about their last tour together. It was March of 1988. Frank had said that Sammy was sixty-two, and he's the kid. Frank was seventy-two and Dean was seventy. Frank said at their ages the only annual event they could hope for was their birthdays. But Frank

and my father were determined to do a final tour, and it was all in an effort to save their buddy Dean. Dean, who always found humor in everything and was extremely funny, had just lost his son, Dean Paul Martin, in a plane crash. He was extremely depressed, in a state like his friends had never seen him. Pop said, "Dean didn't need the money from a final tour, he had plenty, lived humbly, dressed simply." When he would do a show in Vegas, he would bring one tuxedo, one shirt—no makeup, no accessories in his dressing room. The only jewelry he

Mom and Dad enjoying a screening of *Sergeants 3* back in 1961.

wore was a watch he had designed himself and a flashy pinky ring given to him by Frank. Dean was a simple, happy, humorous man until the death of his son. Pop and Frank thought hitting a tour would restore his spirits.

Dean didn't want to do the final tour, but wasn't about to let his buddies down. They held a major press conference with local newspapers, TV networks, radio, magazine, and foreign press. The plan was to do about thirty cities, in two parts. The Rat Pack would work March and April of '88, take a few months off to play Vegas dates, then finish up part two in September and October. Frank, as he often did onstage, told my father to start it off. "Ladies and gentlemen, we thank you for coming here today . . ." and Dean piped in from behind saying, "Is there any way we can call the whole thing off?" The press roared. Pop continued that they wanted to officially announce that they would be together again, the first time since Vegas in the '60s. Frank didn't miss a beat, "And definitely the last time." The press roared. The chemistry, the rapport between Frank, Dean, and Sammy, was back. The love was deep, the humor was there, and the hip banter cheered Dean up, just as they had hoped.

The first two rehearsals were held at my father's house. Pop would say, "Frank, all kidding aside, we still think of you as Chairman of the Board." Dean would respond with, "Yeah, Frank. You're the chairman and we're bored." Or sometimes you would hear my father on a mic offstage after Frank finished a song, "It's wonderful that a man of that age can still sing like that." And Dean would reply, "But let's go out and help him before his oxygen runs out." Dean was smiling, happy, distracted.

By the time they hit New York, the orchestra was rehearsing under Morty Stevens—the crew was back on track. Dean was joking with the stage hands and tech crew about Frank always sticking his finger in his food. He told Frank, "Everything I ate last night tasted like your finger." Frank would play back, poking his finger in something else, "Here, Dean, you should eat this." The clowning was back, and Dean was feeling strong.

At one point Shirley announced to my father that there were not enough black musicians in the orchestra. Frank took control and summoned over the contractor. "What the fuck is this snow-white orchestra? That stinks!" The contractor said it was too late to change them, that it would cost way too much. Frank said, "Bullshit! I want at least thirty percent black musicians. Pay what you have to. Fix it!" That was Frank, always took the bull by the horns.

Throughout the final tour, marquees read, "Frank, Sammy, Dean. SOLD OUT." Dean did not last the entire tour and retired from show business shortly after, but the shows he did perform made the whole tour worth their while. My father and Frank accomplished their goal. They made Dean smile and laugh again, as audiences throughout the country stood up, applauded, and begged for encores. The Rat Pack were like blood brothers who looked out for each other till death do them part.

CHAPTER 4

ICON

Dad stands in front of a poster for
his 1964 Broadway hit *Golden Boy*.

I arrived at Pop's house the next morning, only to find him fast asleep. I sat outside in a chaise lounge with some of Lessie Lee's famous fried chicken and a glass of Coke. I looked around at the plush garden oasis my pop worked so hard for, and thought, "Wow, my father really is a megastar."

At the peak of his career Pop was a living legend, in high demand with a performance schedule that never waned. As one of the world's top nightclub entertainers, my father reveled in the adulation he strove so hard to win.

Between 1961 and 1968 alone, he starred in numerous Rat Pack films as well as other movies, produced sixteen albums that generated at least eight hit singles, and won Emmy nominations for two television variety shows, one entitled, *The Sammy Davis, Jr. Show*. He had first hit Broadway as a star in the 1956 musical *Mr. Wonderful*, then again in 1964 with *Golden Boy*. In 1972, Pop had a hit record with "The Candy Man," and became a star in Las Vegas. All of this and more earned him the nickname "Mr. Show Business."

In *Golden Boy*, Dad played the role of a Harlem prizefighter who breaks out of the projects to become a famous star. The playwright of the original 1937 story was Clifford Odets, who recruited his buddy, William Gibson, to upgrade it to the composition of Charles Strouse and Lee Adams.

Pop hit Broadway with a bang in *Golden Boy*.

TOP: With *Golden Boy* costar Kenneth Tobey

BOTTOM: On stage in *Golden Boy*: Paula Wayne, Kenneth Tobey, Dad, Charles Welch, and Ted Beniades

Pop injured his ankle during the run of *Golden Boy* in 1968 but he went on anyway. Here he is with actors Lon Satton and Gloria de Haven before a performance at the London Palladium.

While my father was starring in the play, my family lived in a plush apartment at 3½ East Ninety-Third Street, just off of Fifth Avenue. My parents enrolled me and Mark at Dalton. Jeff was just a baby. I remember the first day of school and not wanting to let go of my mother's hand. Mom also enrolled me in toddler ballet classes at Juilliard. I ran all over the dance studio. A donkey on my feet, I was more of an athlete than a ballerina, and was delighted when the ballet phase mercifully ceased.

Mom told a story about one Halloween in New York during this time, when she attended a costume party with my father at a nightclub. Pop had never gone trick-or-treating as a child, so celebrating Halloween at a costume party was as close as he would ever get to reliving the "normal" childhood he was deprived of. Pop hired a top makeup artist to turn my mother into Vampira, and Pop into the Hunchback of Notre Dame. Mom said, "the makeup artist was so good, we thought for sure no one would notice us in our disguises." My parents drove to the costume party. Mom had fake blood dripping down her mouth, and a truck driver pulled up at a red light and said, "Hi, Sammy!" Cover blown.

"Hey, Trace Face, you get uglier every time I see you!" Pop said as the nurse assisted him dragging an IV into the chaise lounge next to mine. He had his hand over his trachea tube.

"Well, look who is up? How you feeling today, Pop?" I asked.

"The cancer monster robbed me of my sleep last night, but feeling a bit better today, sweetie. How are you feeling, Pregasuarus?"

"Like a Pregasaurus," I replied.

"I see Lessie Lee hooked you up!" Pop noticed my empty fried chicken plate. "I thought I was the superstar around here, but when people walk in this house, first thing out of their mouths is, 'Hey, Ms. Jackson, whatcha cooking back there?' I say, 'Yeah, she made her fried chicken. Hang on I'll get you some!" Pop laughed.

"Pop, I know you always call Vegas home, Los Angeles your home away from home, but how did you like living in New York when you were on Broadway?" I asked.

"Loved Broadway, but as a Broadway star, in New York, I was not shielded from racism, Trace. It was no longer about beatings like I endured in the military. I was standing in the middle of a social revolution. Posh liberals would accept me into their homes as the 'token colored star' yet come and go talking about how 'spics' have ruined New York. It was a new kind of racism. Social microaggressions.

"Dr. Chester Pierce, a black professor from Harvard Medical said, and I quote: 'The chief vehicle for proracist behaviors are microaggressions. These are subtle, stunning, often automatic, and nonverbal exchanges which are "put-downs" of blacks by offenders.'

"He couldn't be more correct. I attended liberal

Family photos, with Mom and my brother Mark—
our rainbow tribe.

Dad as a guest of Johnny Carson, 1968

Bandleader Sammy Kaye visits Dad backstage at the Majestic Theater during the run of *Golden Boy*, November 1964.

private parties with buffet tables: lobster Newburg, pâté de foie gras, a tin of caviar resting on shaved ice, and then something 'special' for the 'token colored star' . . ."

"Like a platter of fried chicken?" I added.

"And they didn't make it like Lessie Lee or Colonel Sanders either!" Pop chuckled. "There were upper crust restaurants in New York that still wouldn't let me through the front door and Fifth Avenue doormen who turned me away from private parties we were invited to."

"And we lived off Fifth Avenue ourselves."

"Microaggressions. The token liberal line was no longer, 'my best friend is black.' It was: my son goes to school with Dr. Ralph Bunche's son. Both were

lame attempts to make us feel assimilated. Even my own people—the colored press—turned on me, calling me an 'Uncle Tom'—just like they called Dr. Bunche when he was the first black man to win the Nobel Peace Prize. As if we didn't fight any racial battles to become successful. I was living proof that black folks were not the stereotype of a slow, lazy, shuffling Stepin Fetchit. But the black press never appreciated that—just claimed we sold out." Pop shook his head.

"I read a book about Judaism once, and it said: 'The difference between love and hate is understanding.' Unfortunately, for us colored folks the understanding was obstructed by prejudgments without due examination. Hey, if white folks were

Harry Belafonte, Martin Luther King Jr., *Golden Boy* producer Hillard Elkins, and my father in New York, 1965

Pop guest-starred on some of the most popular shows of the '60s, including *I Dream of Jeannie*.

Jerry Lewis, Dad, Hugh Hefner, and Anthony Newley on the short-lived TV show *Playboy After Dark*

so afraid of color, why hit Florida every year and bake in the sun to darken their skin, right?"

"I remember in college reading Marcel Proust," I said.

"Who?"

"A French writer. We had to memorize a quote for my English Literature class. I'll never forget it because it always reminded me of you, Pop," I said. I recited the quote from Proust aloud to my father: 'We pack the physical outline of the creature we see with all the ideas we have already formed about him. . . .'"

"Well, thank God you learned something in college!" Pop said.

"I am the only one in the family to go to college so far."

"I am proud of you, Trace Face. Like this cat Proust was talking about—prejudgments. And during my Broadway days, Lord, did that come into play. I used to run around with George Rhodes like a chicken with my head cut off. We'd go around from one press conference to another, one colored critic to another, one white liberal socialite to another, trying to 'fix' the prejudgments that were

Dad and Lucille Ball in an episode of *Here's Lucy* aptly called, "Lucy and Sammy Davis, Jr."

stacked against me in the press."

"Did it work?" I asked.

"Heck no," Dad said, "The only thing that worked was one day, my father sat me down and said to me with a despairing voice, 'Son, you ain't gonna get away from it till you die.' He was right. The roots of racism were still deeply grounded; the weeds were hacked here and there, but the weeds still grew at a terrorizing pace."

Things became more frightening when my father's grandmother—Mama—passed away during the run of *Golden Boy*. I was quite young, so young. Both Dad and Mom were devastated. Reflecting on this time, my dad said, "Mama was my rock. After my real mother abandoned me as a baby, Mama was everything. I was beyond crushed when she died," Pop said.

"I wish I had been old enough to know her better," I said.

"Mama lived with us on Evanview Drive for a spell back in the day. Then, I bought her Judy Garland's old house in the Hollywood Hills. I didn't buy the house as some contribution to racial harmony—but it was a beautiful extra that the neighbors could see a prosperous black family and say, 'Look, it's not really true that those colored folks live eighty of 'em in a room.'" Pop smiled.

"One Christmas, I walked in with a gift for Mama. I handed her keys to a new car. I said, 'Hold on, Mama, don't move!' I ran outside to open the garage door, all excited to show her the new car. Smeared in paint across the garage door was: 'Merry

ABOVE: My parents in the early '60s

LEFT: *The Hollywood Palace*—Pop sang with Diahann Carroll in a 1968 episode.

Dad's appearance on the controversial TV show *All in the Family* was one of his most memorable. He actually sat in Archie's chair!

Christmas Nigger!' I wasn't surprised, but it broke my heart, truly. I just wanted to see Mama smile that Christmas, that's all," Pop explained with dismay.

"I'm sorry, Pop," I replied.

"One time I was doing some nightclub somewhere and a white supremacist mob was outside chanting, 'Where's that nigger Jew boy?' I walked outside and started to sing 'I've Got You Under My Skin . . .'—danced a lick, killed them with talent!

That's the only way I knew how to fight it."

"I'm proud of you," I said.

Dad said, "My father's voice rings in my ears every single day of my life. I used to call your grandfather 'scrambled eggs'—he shook so much after he got Parkinson's disease. When your grandfather passed, I remember thinking at the funeral, at last, my father is free to be a man, not a colored man, just a man.

Dad and President Nixon. Nixon was signing a
document appointing him to the National Advisory
Council on Economic Opportunity, 1971.

Pop and Richard Nixon in the Oval Office, 1973

ABOVE: With Edward Cox, Tricia Nixon Cox, Julie Nixon Eisenhower, and David Eisenhower, at the Republican National Convention, August 1972

RIGHT: Pop was a gun enthusiast. He even won fast-draw competitions.

"Popsicle, you're not going anywhere. We're kicking this Davis style, remember?" I replied.

"Your grandfather always called you his 'only-est' granddaughter," my father muttered. He was fading.

"I know, Dad."

"Think I'm going to take a quick nap, baby. Gas tank is on low." Pop took his hand off his trachea tube and gently curled up in a ball, closing his eyes.

"I'll be here when you wake," I said.

The most talked-about kiss in television history was delivered by my father on *All in the Family* in 1972. Pop planted a kiss on the right cheek of Archie Bunker, the narrow-minded bigot played by Carroll O'Connor. It was my father who changed the weak script ending, and set the country ablaze, underscoring the hypocrisy of the times.

Dad on *Laugh-In*, one of the most popular TV shows of its day. I thought he
was hilarious in it and he obviously enjoyed himself filming it.

Five years earlier, in 1967, Pop planted one of the first black-white kisses in US television history. NBC broadcast a variety special entitled *Movin' with Nancy.* In addition to the Emmy Award–winning musical performances, the show is notable for Nancy Sinatra and my father greeting each other with a kiss.

In the early 1970s, Pop startled the nation when he physically hugged Republican President Nixon during a live television broadcast. The incident was controversial and Dad received a hostile reaction from his peers. My father also performed on a USO tour of Vietnam at the behest of President Nixon's administration.

I thought about how my father used his talent mixed with kindness to fight prejudice.

My father loved comic and dramatic acting and did so from the '50s on. In the early days, Pop continued to entertain at the country's hottest nightclubs, while taping dramatic roles in two television anthology series, *General Electric Theater* and *Zane Grey Theatre*.

In November 1958, Pop played the role of escaped convict Glenn Griffin in the staged play *The Desperate Hours*. The same year my father was in two feature films: *Anna Lucasta* with Eartha Kitt and Samuel Goldwyn's big-budget production of *Porgy and Bess*, starring Sidney Poitier and Dorothy Dandridge.

On September 9, 1967, a one-time special of *Laugh-In* aired. Pop was comical, dressed in a white wig and black robe, playing a judge. He entered the courtroom saying, "Here comes the judge! Here comes the judge! Order in the court room! Here comes the judge!" My mother got such a kick out of the *Laugh-In* show, she had T-shirts custom-made for me and my brothers to wear on a trip to London with HERE COMES THE JUDGE! printed on the front.

The nurse came out to check on my father and give him his medicine. He woke as she fumbled around with his IV. She asked him how he was feeling and he shrugged.

"You're still here, Trace Face," Pop said.

"Still here, Pop. How are you feeling?" I asked.

"Okay, till that darn nurse woke me up!" he replied.

"So, Pop, tell me, when are you getting rid of that gun collection upstairs? I got a baby on the way here!"

Dad was a sharpshooter and fancy gun spinner. He treasured his gun collection. Pop made appearances in western films and was a guest star in several westerns. He even showed James Dean a few tricks, but always felt guilty after his untimely death that he had ignored him as the weird, quiet kid in the corner at so many of his own private parties.

"Let's not get carried away now. Heck, I won fast-draw competitions. Johnny Cash said I was capable of drawing and firing a Colt Single Action Army revolver in a quarter of a second! My guns are here to stay! Let's change the subject, what else is on your mind?"

"The divorce . . . ," I said.

"From your mom? Such happy thoughts you have on your mind today, Trace Face!" Pop replied.

"I heard Mom's side, but only parts of yours." I looked him straight in the eye, and he knew I was serious.

"Oh God! Haven't we been through that?" Pop shrugged.

"Well?" I asked.

"I just couldn't be what she wanted me to be, Trace Face."

"What was that?"

"A family man. My performance schedule was rigorous. I was moving at a breakneck pace. I've said it before and I'll say it again. I had perhaps an unhealthy commitment to show business—for me,

ABOVE: Even when he was "off" at parties, Pop loved to entertain.

BELOW: Laughing it up with photographer Milton Greene and Marilyn Monroe.

there was always another mountain to climb, another movie to do, another place to play. I gotta be the biggest, I gotta be a star, a megastar—in the meantime, your mother and you kids were suffering."

"You missed a lot of our childhood, Pop," I said.

"And every time I would get a guilt feeling, I'd play 'Father Knows Best' for two weeks out of a year. What kind of life was that? Finally, your mom, who went through so much pain because of me, who I am delighted to have remained dear friends with, told me, 'I can't take this anymore and I never want to get to the point that I hate you. You are a good person just pointed in another direction,'" Pop explained.

"She understood," I said.

"Your mother did a remarkable job raising you kids; you are super kids. I am thrilled to finally have a relationship with each of you, based on honesty. But back in the day, I was like a mouse caught in a habit trail; I couldn't get off the treadmill. The wheel just kept spinning. Naturally, everything was taken care of for your mother financially. That was my saving grace—I provided for my family," Pop said.

At the Mayfair Hotel in London, 1966, Dad reads a newspaper that claimed his marriage to my mother was headed for a divorce. He tossed it in the air to show what he thought of that!

"And your mother let me see you whenever I wanted. But it was when I was in town, which wasn't that often. I was working forty weeks a year because that was my need, to work. See, I always needed to work. It was ingrained in me from the day I started show business at three years old. Work, work, work. Not to mention that I was spending more than I was making. Really, I was a fool, in my book. But that was me. I realized it too late."

"I always thought the divorce was because Uncle Frank was divorcing Mia Farrow at the same time?" I joked.

"Ha. Trace, I loved your mom. Always will. In '66, I even named a little recording company after her: MBD for May Britt Davis," Pop said lovingly.

"I remember your mother announced to the Las Vegas press that we would do a trial separation after seven years of marriage. The press hounded me with questions. All I could tell them was 'May told me she wanted a trial separation, and I must admit it comes as a big blow to me.' I was hoping we could reconcile, but deep down I knew it was futile," Pop said sadly.

Mom and Dad were very close. When Dad dragged the divorce on for months—his lawyers refusing to answer any calls—it was because he never wanted to divorce my mother. "I was hoping she would change her mind," he always told us.

"I moved out and left her with you kids in the old Selznick estate for a spell. Later, I moved the family down the street to a house I bought your mother on Angelo Drive around Benedict Canyon Drive. I moved into this house, 1151 Summit Drive. I bought me a house on Harridge Drive at the top of Summit, too, you know," Pop said.

"But we grew up in Lake Tahoe," I said.

"We vacationed there every summer. Your mother loved Lake Tahoe, it reminded her of Sweden. By 1970, your mother felt it was important to move to a quiet place where you children could see me as much as possible. Your Mom chose to raise you there, knowing that—two times a year, for extended runs—I would do a show in Tahoe and two in Reno, in addition to trips to Vegas and vacations. I got myself one of those Harrah's villas in Tahoe for a spell, but it was so quiet there by the lake. Do you remember how I hated that place?"

"Too peaceful for a city boy?" I chuckled.

"No joke. So I moved to the sixteenth floor of the Harrah's hotel, the 'Sammy Davis, Jr. Suite,'" Pop explained. "Your Mom was kind enough to let me move Lessie Lee into this house here on Summit Drive—so when you kids came down from Tahoe to visit, you would have a nanny. She said, I needed a nanny more than she did." Pop chuckled. "I imagine I did."

"Lessie Lee loves it here because she has her own quarters," I said.

"Uh-huh," Pop impersonated Lessie Lee. We both laughed.

"I remember Lessie Lee flew everywhere with us on vacations. If I was scared she would lay in bed with me. What a gem," I added. "You know, Pop,

Mom never said a bad word about you after the divorce."

In a three-minute hearing on December 19, 1968, Mom got an uncontested divorce in Santa Monica Superior Court." She told Judge Ritterband, "I asked my husband to stay home but he never could because of his hectic schedule. There was no family life to speak of." She was awarded custody of the children. I was seven; Mark, eight; and Jeff, four.

Over the years Pop recounted to me and in many published interviews, that it took him years to do a 360, to watch his life change, come around and realize, "Boy, I'll never make that mistake again." When my parents were married and my brothers and I were young, Dad was one of the most famous and in-demand entertainers in the world. We didn't stand a chance. At that time in his life, he just felt this intense desire to get out there and be the best.

Dame Margot Fontayn hands Pop a mini statue (of himself!) as a thank you from the Royal Academy of dancing in 1968.

NEXT SPREAD: My father in his element, singing and dancing. He gave everything in him to each performance.

Being the best had always been his best weapon to fight ignorance and intolerance. He had to keep going.

"See, if I walked on the stage," Pop told me, "I could fight the prejudice in everyone's mind—that was my thinking. Boy, I'll stay out here till I get ya. In Vegas, I would do a two-and-a-half-hour show and think nothing of it. Folks in the audience were looking at their watches. The manager would tell me, they don't come to see you; they come to gamble, so get off the stage! Ha! I didn't even realize the time passing. I had captured my audience and gained their respect. Then, after the show, I still felt the need to keep the audience—have a big party, have them around me."

"By the late '80s, everything changed. My great joy in life was to go home, have Altovise fix me a little something, warm up some soup or something in the kitchen, lie with my feet up, grab my clicker, and talk back to the television. *Click, click, click*. Now that is joy. Pure joy!" Pop laughed.

Whenever Dad came to Tahoe or Reno for work, Mom was there. She would go with friends to see my father's show. Dad frequently hung around our house with good friends—the Apocotos' and Louise Hames. Mom looked forward to my father coming and so did we. During each visit, Mom would go off and have dinner alone with Dad. I caught a glimpse once backstage in the dressing room and my father had his hand on Mom's cheek. I will never forget the look he gave her. Everyone should have someone look at them like that—just once. Although she had

many offers, Mom did not remarry for twenty years after the divorce and three years after my father's death.

"Pop, you know, in Lake Tahoe, we were the only black kids at our school for quite some time. But it was a different time. We actually made lifelong friends there," I said.

"Remember how I would tease you—'how's life in Shangri-La'?" Pop joked.

"Life was good in Shangri-La, Pop. We missed you, though." I smiled.

"Do you remember when I worked a show at Harrah's with Bill Cosby? Before the show, Bill asked me to do some impersonations. He wanted to throw this joke on the stage: 'Sam, you were wonderful, don't you do any people that's alive?' " Pop laughed.

"That's when I realized most of the great actors I impersonated were in heaven. From then on, I cut down on my impersonations in a major way; I just can't impersonate the young entertainers of your generation—Michael Jackson, maybe, but that's it," Pop explained.

"All I recall is that you were always working. Mom said during the marriage, you were so busy she started to pick up painting. Benay Venuta gave her fine art lessons at home, did you know that?" I said.

"Yes. Your mother was and is a fine abstract painter. As for me, even when I wasn't working, I was attending award shows, making appearances. The year we divorced, in 1968, I remember I won the Spingarn Medal from the NAACP for my efforts

Dad won an Emmy Award for his TV special *The Swinging World of Sammy Davis, Jr.*, 1966

My dad's performance of "Rhythm of Life" was a show-stopper in *Sweet Charity*, 1969.

against racism. There was always something," Pop replied.

There was always something for Pop. Simply helping out his fellow black performers was a top priority. Claude Trenier, of the Trenier Brothers song-and-dance ensemble said, "Sammy was doing things to help the black cause. But because he wasn't 'Right on' and what's called the 'fists in the air' and all that stuff, they thought he wasn't into it.

But he was into it deep. He was black and he knew he was black, so he tried to help other blacks. He said to our group, 'You want to go to Carnegie Hall with me?' I said, 'Sure!' We went and played in Carnegie Hall. How many acts dying to get into Carnegie Hall? And he took us in there with him." That was my father. A giver.

"But why marry Altovise two years after divorcing Mom?" I said, getting us back on track.

On the set of *Sweet Charity* with screenwriter Peter Stone

Taking pictures was one of Pop's favorite hobbies.

Pop, Harry Belafonte, Sidney Poitier, and Quincy Jones in Las Vegas, 1970

"I feel a little guilty about Altovise. Although I was clean at the time, we entertained many guests who were not on the straight and narrow. She was surrounded by alcohol and drugs. She just fell into it. I felt responsible, you know?" Pop said.

"I'll never forget when you told us kids you were going to marry Altovise. My brothers and I came to visit you here, sat down at the dining room table. We saw this strange woman at the table. We looked at each other wondering—who is this lady? Out of nowhere, you introduced us and announced that you were going to marry this total stranger!"

"I didn't handle it well. I'm sorry. I'll never forget your face, Trace; you wouldn't eat!" Pop said.

"When we got home that night we asked Mom why she didn't tell us Pop was getting married? Poor Mom didn't even know about it. She was livid!" I exclaimed.

"It was wrong. Your Mom got so upset. And Lord, when she was mad she would slip into her heavy Swedish accent and mispronounce everything—kind of comical her decoding process. She kept saying to me, 'You have kids at dining table and have them walk into some kind of trappings?' Good Lord. I apologized, but I don't think she ever forgave me," Pop explained.

On May 11, 1970, Reverend Jesse Jackson married my father and Altovise Gore in a Philadelphia courthouse. Altovise Gore was a former dancer in *Golden Boy*. They adopted a son, Manny, in 1989 and remained married until Dad's death in 1990. Her drinking got so heavy, when Pop got sick with throat cancer, he locked her out of his master wing of the house.

"When I married Altovise in May of 1970, my schedule was insane. In addition to nightclub acts and television appearances, my manager, Sy Marsh, decided my records were not selling well enough on Frank's Reprise label. Although I had a #1 hit on the Easy Listening Singles chart with 'I've Gotta Be Me' in 1969—Sy thought it was time to pull in a more hip, younger audience. We signed with Berry Gordy at Motown one month before the wedding," Pop explained.

I added: "I remember reading about the Motown gig, Pop. Sy said, 'the world's number one record producer, who's black, has signed the world's greatest entertainer, who's also black.'"

"Two black cats made in heaven—I wish."

Gordy told Sy he didn't think Pop had the Motown sound. They got out of the deal, left Motown. He did a studio album with MGM, and in June 1972, "The Candy Man" became his signature song. For three weeks it placed #1 on the *Billboard* Hot 100 list.

"Pop, how did you ever find time for your hobbies, like your photo work or watching daytime soaps?" I asked my dad.

"There's a lot of sit-around-and-wait time in Hollywood, you know. I always loved to take photos of the family, of friends. Jerry Lewis gave me my first important camera, my first 35 millimeter, during the Ciro's period—early '50s. He hooked me. Later on I would use a medium format camera. The nice thing

about being an avid photographer is that nobody interrupts a man taking a picture to ask, 'What's that nigger doin' here?'" Pop explained.

Pop's photo work was compiled in a book by Burt Boyar published in 2007, titled, *Photo by Sammy Davis, Jr.* In the book are rare photos of Robert Kennedy, Jackie Kennedy, and Martin Luther King. Intimate shots of close friends like Frank Sinatra, Dean Martin, Marilyn Monroe, Jerry Lewis, Nat King Cole, and even James Dean are in the book. There are pictures of his father dancing with Will Mastin and beautiful snapshots of the family, my white mom and her three black kids bouncing about. It is a lovely photographic representation of Pop's life and his favorite off-stage-and-screen hobby.

Joey Heatherton, Frank Sinatra, my father, and Edie Adams on a '60s TV special.

Pop sure had style! Here he is performing in London in January 1973.

CHAPTER 5

ELDER STATESMAN

My dad, an elder statesman of the
entertainment industry, in the early '80s

My father looked gaunt, tired. "Want me to help you to bed, Pop? Maybe you can catch a *General Hospital* rerun," I said.

"I loved being on that show," Pop whispered. He was falling fast asleep—until Altovise's dogs came flying out of the house, jumped all over him, and got tangled in his medical tubes.

Pop was livid, "I'm a superstar, you f'in dogs! See, Trace, no one pays me any attention!" We both laughed. "Don't make me laugh, Trace Face!" I called the strong and loving Lessie Lee to help me with the dogs and to take Pop in.

"Pop, remember when you won that Daytime Emmy Award for *One Life to Live*? [In which he had a recurring role.]," I said as we climbed my father and his IV up to his bedroom.

"I was nominated, never won, that was 1980. But I loved that show, too. Also nominated but never won for *The Cosby Show* in 1987," Pop said as we tucked him into bed and turned on the television.

My father loved game shows, too. He appeared on *Family Feud* in 1979 on ABC. He made a cameo on *Card Sharks* in 1981 on NBC. He and Altovise

Dad, Princess Grace, and Cary Grant in 1971

Dad, Liza, and Frank doing promo for their "comeback" concert, 1989

also appeared as panelists on *Tattletales* in the 1970s.

In the 1980s, Pop performed in the *Cannonball Run* movies and continued his stage and film work. But after his hip surgery in the late 1980s, my father started to slow down. He was last seen onstage with Uncle Frank and Liza Minnelli in *The Ultimate Event*. In 1989, my father made his final film, *Tap*, which was a tribute to the legends of the tap dancing era.

I sat with my father as he fell asleep with the television on full blast. I watched him sleep and thought about all the wonderful trips we had gone on together after his divorce from my mother. Monaco, in the south of France, was the most memorable.

Monaco was the most beautiful place my husband and I had ever seen. Pop's rules were simple: "You and Guy get here, and I will take care of everything else." We happily agreed.

Upon arrival we were whisked to Monte Carlo through a tiny winding road of countryside that unfolded into one word: stunning. In the Principality of Monaco, the houses were small yet grand, the Côte d'Azur spectacular and, of course, the Palace. It didn't seem quite real. Someone lives there? Holy cow!

We arrived at the Hôtel de Paris. I had stayed in some ritzy hotels but this one took the cake. The awe-inspiring lobby with crystal chandeliers and marble colonnades spoke of majestic sovereignty.

Performing with two of his favorite people, Frank Sinatra and Liza Minnelli, in 1989

Cannonball Run II: Burt Reynolds, Dean Martin, Shirley MacLaine, Dad, and Frank Sinatra

Our room overlooked the plaza with a panoramic view of the Casino de Monte-Carlo. The Casino was designed by Charles Garnier, the architect of the Paris Opera House with beautiful frescoes and stained-glass windows. The Casino de Monte-Carlo was a far cry from the "anything goes" Las Vegas casinos. We would sit on the balcony and watch people come and go night after night, dressed to the nines.

Dad's suite at the Hôtel de Paris, oh my gosh! It overlooked the entire French Riviera and the Prince's palace. Breathtaking. We sat out on the bal-cony for hours chatting away amidst the royal spirit, glitz, and glamour that was Monaco.

Dad would throw out his infamous joke, "Do you know why I stay in this beautiful hotel?" "No, Pop," I would reply. "Because I can," Pop would say on key. We fell out laughing each and every time. But there was power behind his laugh. Never far from my father's mind was the fact that there was a time when he couldn't stay in beautiful hotels. Not just because of money, but because of the color of his skin. I think Pop always threw out his joke as a way of giving thanks to God.

Dad and Bruce Forsyth got together for an hour-long television special in 1980. Forsyth later said,
"The best TV show I ever did was with Sammy Davis, Jr. I played for him when he sang, he played for me when
I sang, and when people come to visit now and I show them the tape, it still stands up as a good show."

I thought this was one of Pop's funniest TV appearances—
on *The Jeffersons* (with Isabel Sanford) in 1984.

Dad performed in Monaco and brought down the house. We were invited to the palace for dinner after the show. Wow, you cannot overdress for a dinner at the palace. It was about two in the morning, I think. Tiny tealight candles lit the path we strolled down. We dined outside, French Riviera style with Prince Rainier, Princess Caroline, Lynn Wyatt, a socialite from Texas, and other notable guests.

I sat next to Princess Caroline. I still struggle to describe my awe. I say it to this day—she was the most beautiful woman I have ever seen—her skin, her eyes, just striking. When I saw Princess Caroline, I thought, there are women and there are

ladies. She was a lady in the true definition of the word.

Princess Caroline spoke perfect French and English, and who knows how many other languages. She was so composed at the table, such a fine hostess, made each guest feel special, like she had known us for years. Princess Caroline had a way of involving her guests in conversation that was beyond skilled; it was a true talent.

She asked me, "You and your husband have been together a long time. Are you thinking of children?" I stammered. How do you reply to a princess? Umm, oh don't say umm, I thought. She sensed me lost in her charming spell, and gracefully broke in, "There is never a perfect time for children—just have them, treasure them." All I could think of was, *okay, Princess, yes Princess*, so I nodded politely.

Another memorable trip I took with my father and my husband was to the White House in 1987. My father was the recipient of a Kennedy Center Honor. At the ceremony he would be honored by his closest friends, including Lucille Ball, who had come to the house over the years for my father's home-cooked gourmet meals.

Dad had slept at the White House previously, as a guest under former President Nixon. Pop has been credited by the Nixon administration for what is now a tradition, the POW dinner. In 1987, he headed back to the White House, as a guest of President Ronald Reagan and Vice President George H. W. Bush. The Kennedy Center Honors would be a three-day extravaganza. My father could not have been more proud.

We arrived in Washington aboard Bill Cosby's Gulf Stream jet, the *Camille*, named after his wife. Mr. Cosby had loaned his jet to Dad for the occasion, staffed with a private chef. From Van Nuys, California, we flew to St. Louis, where my father had to perform, then on to D.C. We flew by the beautiful arch. When I told Pop I didn't see it too well, he had the pilot circle again. Pretty cool.

In D.C., my father gave us our own limo. He wanted a driver to take us wherever we wanted to tour for the duration of the stay. The driver took my

husband and me to the Ritz-Carlton hotel, where Kennedy Center honorees and other guests were gathered. You could not walk anywhere in the Ritz without bumping into someone famous—it was surreal. Soon it was time for the main event.

"Can't be late," Dad always said, "it's bad form." Driving up to the White House, we were nervous. The protocol alone scared us, not to mention the security and receiving line. There was a cocktail party for Dad and other Kennedy Center honorees in the East Room, including the great Bette Davis, who was so beautiful. My husband and I were the only ones that weren't famous. The pristine food spread was incredible. The president and first lady greeted each honoree privately, in a separate room.

Dad returned to the cocktail party after the private greeting. He was having a great time when he noticed a group of black guys that were peering out of the kitchen. Next thing I know, Dad was gone. Later, we found him in the kitchen, with his bow tie loosened, hanging out with all the folks who had made the evening possible. What else would you expect from Sammy Davis, Jr.? It was a touching moment, but nothing out of the ordinary. It was just Pop.

The evening of the Kennedy Center Honors, my father was beaming. The room was electric. It was not lost on me that it was the "Kennedy" Center: named after the Kennedys, who hurt my father so deeply when he was not invited to the JFK inauguration celebration—after all his hard work performing for the campaign. Ironic, I thought.

One day, we were invited to the State Department for a seated dinner with George Pratt Shultz, former US Secretary of State under Reagan. We rode in separate limos from the Ritz-Carlton, and pulled up to what I would call Fort Knox security. Once cleared by security, we entered a huge but somehow intimate ballroom with Kennedy Center honorees and other invited guests.

Over dinner, George Shultz spoke about football, the history of the room, and told funny stories about other dinners that put the table guests at ease.

After the State Department dinner, we returned to the Ritz-Carlton. We had drinks at a big table with honorees and guests—everyone laughing and kicking off their shoes, talking about our three-day extravaganza. We went around the room, each of us saying what we were thankful for. No one wanted the evening to end. We returned home on Bill Cosby's *Camille*. Washington, D.C., was sure a once-in-a-lifetime trip.

Back to the reality of sitting by Pop, reminiscing about our travels in my head, as he rested. I told him something like, "I love you, Pop, you are an icon. Your star shines bright on the Hollywood Walk of Fame!"

"Thanks, Trace Face. Just don't let me die here." Pop was referring to his legacy, and keeping it alive. His heavy eyelids closed for the night and I headed home.

Once in my own room, melancholy set in motion. I kept hearing my father's voice, "Just don't let me die here." I closed the blinds to shut out the moonlight and surrendered myself to a state of darkness. Despite my resistance, reality was mounting, and I knew the end was near.

Out of nowhere, I found myself in my Nissan 240SX upside down in an embankment off Tierra Rejada Road, near Thousand Oaks, California. I woke up to someone banging on my window pane. I felt water on my face. Was it raining? Where was I? No, it was not raining; it was blood on my face and I was stuck upside down in my car, pregnant. *Don't let me die*, I thought. *Don't let my baby die.* Bad enough that Pop was dying.

I was driving home from a CSUN Alumni basketball game, listening to "Tears for Fears" on a cassette player, when a big old car on a two-lane road between Simi Valley and Moorpark came smack into my lane. It hit me head on, and I rolled into an embankment, flipping upside down. I was pulled out of the car. It had automatic shoulder restraint seat belts. Luckily, I had forgotten the manual lap belt around my belly, which saved my unborn child's life.

A sheriff's deputy radioed in that "we have a fatality." Paramedics came to the scene. The deputy asked, "Who else was in the car with you?" I replied, "No one. Call my dad." The police asked, "What's his name?" I said, "Sammy Davis, Jr." There was a moment of disbelief, and I said, "Yeah, that's him." I gave up the number. My father was panicked, naturally. I could only imagine Pop hearing the news with flashes of his own nearly fatal car accident that took his eye.

They told my father that they were taking me to Los Robles Hospital and Medical Center. Mom was in Lake Tahoe at the time. Someone phoned her as well. A stranger called my husband, Guy. By the time Guy arrived, there were fire trucks and police cars everywhere. He pushed through the crowd shouting, "That's my wife! That's my wife! She's pregnant!"

My obstetrician, Dr. Karalla, had me stay in the hospital overnight to check on the baby, but I was lucky that other than some minor bruising, we had both survived the crash. I called my father from the hospital, "I can't attend your sixtieth anniversary tribute or I might lose your grandchild, Pop." I told him I was nervous about the baby.

His tribute was only a few days away, but Pop was just relieved that God had worked another miracle in his life and mine. He told me not to worry, that it was good to be nervous—it's a sign that you are alive and well, he said.

He recalled a story when he starred at the Royal

Dad in one of his most unusual roles—in *Alice in Wonderland*, 1985. Natalie Gregory played Alice. He was game for anything!

With Sonia Braga in the 1988 movie *Moon Over Parador*

Albert Hall in London with his two closest friends, Frank Sinatra and Liza Minnelli. It was part of the European leg of "The Ultimate Event" tour. Pop said he was so nervous when he walked into this grand concert hall, it was such a big jump from the Pigalle in the '60s. Dad said he was sweating so much, if he had a piece of soap he could wash his hands. But he remembered what Eddie Cantor once told him, "Son, the day you stop being nervous before you face an audience, get out of the business." "So be nervous, Trace Face," he said, "it will keep you on your toes with the doctors."

Dad was on the upswing despite the cancer ravaging his body. My father taped his sixtieth anniversary tribute before a live audience at the Shrine Auditorium in Hollywood, without me beside him. Dad's lifelong friends paid tribute and celebrated his sixty years in show business. This heartfelt special in his honor aired in April 1990. The show won an Emmy and was my father's last major public appearance.

The tribute included video clips of Pop in show business all the way back to his childhood in vaudeville. Live tributes were performed by celebrity entertainers like Frank Sinatra, Dean Martin, Bill Cosby, Clint Eastwood, George Bush, Ella Fitzgerald, Eddie Murphy, Quincy Jones, Liza Minnelli, Bob Hope, Shirley MacLaine, Goldie Hawn, Whitney Houston, Jesse Jackson, Michael Jackson, and so many more.

There was one particular moment when Gregory Hines finished a tap dancing number, jumped off the

My father and Gregory Hines in a publicity shot for *Tap*, 1989

stage, and kissed my father's shoes, that was very touching. Michael Jackson took the stage with a song he composed just for Pop, "You Were There." It was a song about how my father broke down the walls of racism and opened the door for him and other young artists of color. The utmost respect for my father enthroned Michael's face. The lyrics were so power-

ful; the song sung so deep from within Michael's heart and soul, it made my father tear up in the audience. Pop and Michael were always close. Michael called him Mr. D and used to come by the house, go to the library, and borrow tapes of Pop's shows. He told Pop in Monte Carlo in 1988, "Y'know, I stole some moves from you, the attitudes."

This tribute could not have come at a more perfect time to lift my father's spirits. By this time, Pop knew he didn't have much time left, and to see his closest friends honor his long career was exactly what he needed to close the final chapter of his life.

I was planning to go visit Pop after my baby checkup on April 19, 1990. My son's due date was April 10, so he was already nine days late. I went for my appointment and Dr. Karalla said, "Don't go home." He checked me into Tarzana Regional Medical Center where he would induce labor. My husband, Guy, was by my side the whole time. My mother came before I was given a C-section.

My son, Sam, was born the next day, on April 20, 1990. Not only had God blessed me with a beautiful son, but Pop fought the doctor's odds, and my revelation had indeed come true. Pop was still alive to meet his only blood grandson, named in his honor.

As we waited for the guard to open the gate to my father's home, reporters literally laid on my car, snapping pictures of my husband, myself, and our newborn. We ignored the press, and pulled into Pop's driveway. We grabbed the baby seat with our newborn in it and headed into Pop's house.

We entered from the side entrance since Altovise had been locked out of his 3,400-square-foot master wing. Pop never talked to her. He would just hand her money from time to time.

We went into my father's office, where the crew was gathered: Shirley, David Steinberg (Pop's publicist turned producer), security guards, and Lessie

Lee running the house. Little Sammy was naturally the center of attention, and everyone circled around him and spoke of how beautiful he was.

Pop was prepared that we were coming, so he was out of bed, trachea tube in, medication flowing through his IV, sitting on a huge, cozy chair in his bedroom as we walked in.

I had never seen my father's face so happy as I said, "Hi, Dad" and showed him baby Sammy, half bent over in pain from my C-section. He was elated with tears of happiness, the wonder of it all, that look of "Wow, this is my grandchild." I got so lucky; I had a boy, named him Sammy, and I had him in time for Pop to meet him.

After Sammy's birth, Pop slipped in and out of responsiveness; cancer, bit by bit, robbed him of his life. I remember one day when I was visiting, Pop was lucid enough to say to me, "Trace, I'm scared." I looked at him with watery eyes and said, "Me, too, Pop."

The next time, my husband and I were visiting, the nurse was changing Pop's sheets. My husband held Pop like a baby, softly kissing his forehead. From that moment on, my father was our hero. In his deteriorating state, he was a distinguished man, the finest I had ever seen. He rendered himself even more worthy of our regard. Guy gently put Dad down on the bed, into fresh linens, carefully, very carefully as just a gentle rub on his skin was painful. Time passed and his condition grew worse. From some vegetative state of half memory, Pop could still feel pain, and would wince if he was touched. There was no coming back from this. By the next visit, Pop couldn't speak at all. From his eyes, you could tell he wasn't all together there anymore. Was he in a coma? I don't know.

Liza Minnelli was one of the few friends on Pop's "OKAY Guest List" that he would allow to see him in his current condition. My father and Liza had been close pals for years. The day she came to the house, she knew it was a final good-bye, that this was the last time she would see my father alive.

Liza had covered a show in Lake Tahoe for my father when he first got the sore throat that was later diagnosed as cancer. It was August of 1989. Little did I suspect that this would signal the beginning of the end of my father's life. "I got a little tickle, Trace, not doing the show tonight. Wanna come up to the suite?" Pop said over the phone. I was on my way. Pop and I had reconnected, and become true pals at my bachelorette party in Vegas. My bachelorette party was filled with champagne, jokes, laughs, and lots of stories with my friend Julie Clark, the McGuire sisters, Pop, and Frank Sinatra. It could not have been more perfect. I treasure those moments every day.

I went to my father's suite at Harrah's in Lake Tahoe with my friend Diane. I asked Dad what was wrong. He said, "Just a sore throat, no biggie." My father couldn't do the show that night. So of course, who comes in early to cover? Good ole Liza. What a kind, gracious soul. She did the show in a sweater and jeans—her luggage hadn't arrived yet.

By the time Liza was done, the entire audience was in her hand. They had come to see Dad, a line wrapping around the casino, but Liza had taken them over. The result was pure magic. I thought, *That* is why Liza is a star. Forget that she was the child of Hollywood royalty. A talent and personality all her own made her a star. At the end of the show, Liza announced that Dad was truly sorry for missing the performance. Liza was a class act all the way. She and my father were a bona fide force of professional habit, captivating audiences with a mere glance all over the world—and best buddies to boot.

I went home late that night to Mom's house in Tahoe. Something was bugging me; I didn't know what, but something was bothering me. I tried to shrug it off, but it lingered in the distance, I just couldn't shake it. Pop said he was going to be fine. He had never lied to me, so why didn't I believe him?

I knew something was off but found solace in knowing that he was going to get a checkup, just to make sure. He was a singer and a smoker. He had sore throats before. Trace, I said to myself, stop. Just stop. But it stuck with me, the frailty of his condition. I felt uneasy.

I was right to worry, I would later learn. There was a node, a little something. Not a big deal. "May have a little surgery," Pop said on the phone. It came slamming into reality. *I have to get to Pop. I have to look at him, face to face. I would know then.* I got in my car and drove to him. There he was. Alone, not unusual, I thought, but then it hit me. No cigarettes, no ash tray, no nothing.

Dad in *Tap*, 1989

A tribute to the great musical numbers in films of the past, *That's Dancing!*, 1985

Pop tried to cover, but I knew we were in for a fight. I wanted answers. For better or worse, I got them. The sore throat had turned into a node and the node into cancer. Could this really be happening to my father? *What now?* I thought. Dad started his radiation. He was tired but he was strong, and even maintained his sense of humor. He had developed a bright red area on his neck. It was well known that he loved his Strawberry Crush. He said the red spot on his neck was from drinking so much of it; it finally leaked out. I laughed, but there is was. Cancer.

Liza had been there from the start, from the sore throat in Lake Tahoe, and now she was doing the death march with us. As Liza headed up the stairs to Pop's bedroom, she had to stop on the huge landing and sit on the couch. She was scared to go up. She wanted to know every detail about his condition. "Trace Face, how bad is it? What does he look like?"

One question after another I answered to soothe her nerves, but it was clear that her anticipation was worse than actually seeing Pop would be.

When Liza saw my father, she kissed him, told him she loved him, and left. As I walked her out, she said seeing Pop "was heavy." My father's state was weighing on us all, family and close friends.

About a month after little Sammy was born, I was in Dad's bedroom. I kept remembering what my

Dad and Liza Minnelli, 1990. He's holding his American Dance Honor.

Pop arrived in style at the Royal Albert Hall for one of his final performances, in 1989.

father had said a few months before: "I will live to see my grandson, and after that I have nothing left to live for."

I leaned down and whispered in his ear, "Dad, it's okay if you have to die. It's okay. It'll be okay. I remember everything you said. And I'll take care of it, I promise." I was referring to keeping his legacy alive. "I love you, Popsicle." I kissed my father on his forehead and held his hand. I could feel his thumb brush against mine, so I knew he heard me. He gave me three tiny little squeezes. It was noticeable and deliberate, not an instinct.

Since my father was a megastar, we'd grown used to the press swarming about, but the whole family had been taught a code when we were young by our mother. The code was, if anything was up, squeeze Mom or Dad's hand three times. Pop was not able to say anything back, but he squeezed my hand three times. That was enough for me.

My father died the next morning in his home at 5:56 am, on May 16, 1990. He was sixty-four years old. His funeral was held at the Forest Lawn Memorial Park in Glendale, California. Being Jewish, the family did not want a viewing. We knew Pop would never want one. We were overruled by Altovise, now his widow, who insisted on having a wake with an open casket.

I refused to go to the wake, but would attend the funeral. I sent my husband, Guy, to the wake. Guy told me a photographer was taking pictures of my father in his casket. Appalled, I reached out to Shirley, who asked David Steinberg to do something

about it. David threatened the photographer—told him that Frank Sinatra was so angry he was planning to have a contract put out on his life—if he didn't hand over the film. It wasn't true, but the photographer surrendered the film.

My father was generous to a fault. He left the bulk of his money to Altovise and trusts for his children. There was also an auction where a pair of his tap shoes sold for $11,000 among other memorabilia. His entire estate, property, house, gun collection, art, and memorabilia valued between six and eight million dollars.

People from all over the world, of all races and religions, mourned Dad's death. Fans celebrated his life as the heavyweight champion of the entertainment world. Thousands stood in the roadway from my father's house to Forest Lawn Memorial Park, clapping, shouting, and tipping their hats as the hearse and our limo motorcade drove by. I noted one fan even shaved words into his hair: LUV YOU SAMMY. Lessie Lee rode in the motorcade of limos with us, in a hat with short veil, a pocketbook, and all the trimmings of Southern style respect.

Out in Las Vegas, the lights on the Strip were darkened for ten minutes in honor of Sammy Davis, Jr.—an event that had only happened before for the deaths of President John F. Kennedy and Martin Luther King Jr. Performers, entertainers, celebrities, family, and close friends eulogized him. Publications, some of which had criticized my father during his career, published glowing obituaries. *Ebony* magazine would write a tribute to Dad that through living his life, "the entertainer wrote the Fourteenth Amendment of Show Business." Given Dad's legacies, *Ebony* continued on and I quote, "Sammy Davis, Jr. established racial and religious tolerance in the entertainment industry."

Reverend Jesse Jackson held the funeral service at Forest Lawn. He spoke of Sammy Davis, Jr. and said: "In this one person, black and white, east and west, find common ground. In this one person, African Americans and Jews find common ground." His tribute to my father warmed our hearts. He referred to my father as "Mr. Bojangles" and asked the crowd to stand as he played a recording of Pop singing the song. I cried until I had no more tears left in me.

My Dad left the world of show business bereft of a pioneer whose vast talent shined in the face of racial adversity and opened the door for so many upcoming artists of color. Sammy Davis, Jr. touched generations of performers—beyond color barriers—with his talent and determination.

To me, the greatest relief I felt when Dad died was that the satellite trucks and reporters that were staked outside of his house on the narrow Summit Drive would leave. They had come one by one like buzzards to a carcass. This was pre-Twitter and still the press knew everything.

Now it was over. The trucks were backing away and packing up. Reporters left. The circus was leaving town and that could only mean one thing. Dad really was dead. He was? Yes, he was. Throughout this last personal journey with my father, the doc-

tors told me that he would not recover from cancer, but I never really believed it. He had triumphed over so much adversity in his life, surely he would beat this.

In a way I was angry. Even at my own father. A smoker, no—a lifetime smoker. It had killed him. I still couldn't entirely accept it. One time I found myself driving up to his house on Summit out of mere habit, arrived at the gate, only to realize what I had done, and turned the car around. I fought with God in my car. Please, I begged God, give me one word, one sign, that would ease my fear of living without my father. I tried to fix my thoughts on the future, my beautiful newborn son, my husband, anything that would carry me across this bridge, over this terrifying abyss, to a place where thoughts were beautiful again.

I wanted to be smack in the middle of Pop's lavish emerald gardens with pungent eucalyptus trees and a sparkling pool. I wanted to be in a tranquil oasis where I could drink in the air and extract words, memories, stories, laughter, anything that would make me smile. Then, it came to me. I thought of what my pop would say at one of his private parties: "Leave while you're still interesting, baby." Somehow, someway, I cracked a smile and made my peace with Pop's death.

Today, it is twenty-four years since my father passed. I still struggle with his loss at times. I recently wrote a "Final Good-Bye" letter to Pop after visiting him at Forest Lawn cemetery:

Dear Pop,

Oh my gosh, how you are missed. So many things to talk about and so many things left to be said. You taught me not to worry if I was a round peg in a square hole. You taught me to make my own hole. Who cares, you said.

I wish you could see all my children, Pop. I have four now, two boys and two girls. Sammy named after you, Montana Rae, Chase, and Greer. Remember when you said you were going to be the best grandpa ever? They missed that. But not to worry, Pop, I teach my kids about you all the time, bet you know that right?

I didn't always realize it but I was the luckiest little girl and I am so happy you are my father. Brought up by two parents who looked racism in the eye and laughed at it—who built a cocoon for us, taught us to love no matter what. I must keep the legacy of your talent, determination, generosity, and love alive. I'm working on a new book about you that I hope will do just that.

I gotta go now, Pop. You're my hero.

I will talk to you tonight, forever, for always, for love.
—Me

My brother Mark and I taking a swim with our father, 1966.

SAMMY DAVIS, JR. DISCOGRAPHY

Starring Sammy Davis, Jr. (1955)

Just for Lovers (1955)

Mr. Wonderful (1956)

Here's Looking at You (1956)

Sammy Swings (1957)

It's All Over but the Swingin' (1957)

Boy Meets Girl (1957)

Mood to Be Wooed (1958)

All The Way . . . and Then Some! (1958)

Sammy Davis, Jr. at Town Hall (1959)

Porgy and Bess (1959)

Sammy Awards (1960)

I Gotta Right to Swing (1960)

Mr. Entertainment (1961)

The Wham of Sam! (1961)

Sammy Davis, Jr. Belts the Best of Broadway (1962)

The Sammy Davis, Jr. All-Star Spectacular (1962)

What Kind of Fool Am I—and Other Show-Stoppers (1962)

As Long as She Needs Me (1963)

Sammy Davis, Jr. at the Cocoanut Grove (1963)

Forget-Me-Nots for First Nighters (1963)

Sammy Davis, Jr. Salutes the Stars of the London Palladium (1964)

The Shelter of Your Arms (1964)

California Suite (1964)

Sammy Davis, Jr. Sings the Big Ones for Young Lovers (1964)

When the Feeling Hits You! (1965)

If I Ruled the World (1965)

The Nat King Cole Songbook (1965)

Sammy's Back on Broadway (1965)

Our Shining Hour (1965)

Try a Little Tenderness (1965)

The Sammy Davis, Jr. Show (1966)

The Sounds of '66 (1966)

Sammy Davis, Jr. Sings and Laurindo Almeida Plays (1966)

That's All! (1966)

Sammy Davis, Jr. Sings the Complete Dr. Dolittle (1967)

Lonely Is the Name (1968)

I've Gotta Be Me (1968)

Sammy Davis, Jr.'s Greatest Hits: The Top Twelve (1968)

The Goin's Great (1969)

Something for Everyone (1970)

Sammy Davis, Jr. Now (1972)

Portrait of Sammy Davis, Jr. (1972)

Sammy Davis, Jr. & Count Basie (1973)

That's Entertainment! (1974)

The Song and Dance Man (1976)

In Person '77 (1977)

Hearin' Is Believin' (1979)

Hello Detroit (1984)

FEATURE FILM CREDITS

Rufus Jones for President

A Vitaphone Short (1933)
Released by Warner Bros.

CAST: Sammy Davis (Rufus Jones); Ethel Waters (Mother of Rufus); with: Hamtree Harrington; Dusty Fletcher; Edgar Connor; the Will Vodery Girls; The Russell Wooding Jubilee Singers; and Russell Wooding

CREDITS: Roy Mack (director); A. Dorian Otvos and Cyrus Wood (story and screenplay); E. B. DuPar (photography); Cliff Hess (musical score)

RUN TIME: 21 minutes

Seasoned Greetings

A Vitaphone Short (1933)
Released by Warner Bros.

CAST: Lita Grey Chaplin (Lita Chaplin); Sammy Davis (Henry Johnson); Carleton Macy (J. Beetle); George Haggerty (Parky); Harlan Briggs (Uncle Ben Jones); Robert Cummings (Lita's Beau); with: the Sizzlers; and the Village Barn Hill Billies

CREDITS: Roy Mack (director); A. Dorian Otvos and Cyrus Wood (story and screenplay); E. B. DuPar (photography)

RUN TIME: 20 minutes

Sweet and Low

A Paramount Short (1947)
Released by Paramount Pictures

CAST: Richard Webb (Tom Mather); Catherine Craig (Andrea Mather); Karolyn Grimes (Tammie); Griff Barnett (Harlan Kane); Laura Corbay (Specialty Dancer); Maurice J. McLoughlin (The Great Navarro); Bob Parker (Robert Parker); Will Maston (Leader, the Will Maston Trio); Sammy Davis Sr. (Member, Will Maston Trio); Sammy Davis, Jr. (Member, Will Maston Trio)

CREDITS: Harry Grey (producer); Jerry Hopper (director); Jack Roberts (story and screenplay); Stuart Thompson (photography); Van Cleave (musical score); Billy Daniels (choreographer); Natalie Kalmus (Technicolor consultant); Everett Douglas (editor)

RUN TIME: 19 minutes

Meet Me in Las Vegas

A Metro-Goldwyn-Mayer Production (1956)
Released by Loews Inc.

CAST: Dan Dailey (Chuck Rodwell); Cyd Charisse (Maria Corvier); Agnes Moorehead (Miss Hattie); Lili Darvas (Seri Hatvany); Jim Backus (Tom Culdane); Oscar Karlweis (Lotzi); Liliane Montevecchi (Lili); Cara Williams (Kelly Donovan); George Kerns (Young Groom); Sammy Davis, Jr. (Narrator, "Frankie and Johnny")

CREDITS: Joe Pasternak (producer); Roy Rowland (director); Isobel Lennart (story and screenplay); Robert Bronner (photography); George Stoll (musical score); Hermes Pan (dance director); Cedric Gibbons and Urie McCleary (art directors); Dr. Wesley C. Miller (sound); Albert Akst (editor)

RUN: 111 minutes

Anna Lucasta

A Longridge Enterprises Inc. Production (1959)
Released by United Artists

CAST: Eartha Kitt (Anna Lucasta); Frederick O'Neal (Frank); Henry Scott (Rudolph Slocum); Rex Ingram (Joe Slocum); James Edwards (Eddie); Isabelle Cooley (Katie Lucasta); Rosetta Le Noire (Stella); Georgia Burke (Theresa Lucasta); Claire Leyba (Blanche); Sammy Davis, Jr. (Danny Johnson)

CREDITS: Sidney Harmon (producer); Arnold Laven (director); Philip Yordan (screenplay), from the play *Anna Lucasta* by Philip Yordan; Lucien Ballard (photography); Elmer Bernstein (musical score); John S. Poplin Jr. (art director); Jack Solomon (sound); Richard C. Meyer and Robert Lawrence (editors)

RUN TIME: 97 minutes

Porgy and Bess

Samuel Goldwyn Productions, Inc. (1959)
Released by Columbia Pictures

CAST: Sidney Poitier (Porgy); Dorothy Dandridge (Bess); Sammy Davis, Jr. (Sportin' Life); Pearl Bailey (Maria); Brock Peters (Crown); Leslie Scott (Jake); Diahann Carroll (Clara); Ruth Attaway (Serena); Claude Akins (Detective); Clarence Muse (Peter)

CREDITS: Samuel Goldwyn (producer); Otto Preminger (director); N. Richard Nash (screenplay); from the opera by George and Ira Gershwin and Dubose Heyward, which was based on the play *Porgy* by Dubose and Dorothy Heyward; Leon Shamroy (photography); music by George Gershwin, lyrics by Ira Gershwin and Dubose Heyward (musical score); Andre Previn (arranger); Hermes Pan (dance director); Serge Krizman, Oliver Smith, and Joseph C. Wright (art directors); Fred Hynes (sound); Daniel Mandell (editor)

RUN TIME: 146 minutes

Ocean's Eleven

A Dorchester Production (1960)
Released by Warner Bros.

CAST: Peter Lawford (Jimmy Foster); Frank Sinatra (Danny Ocean); Dean Martin (Sam Harmon); Henry Silva (Roger Corneal); Norman Fell (Peter Rheimer); Clem Harvey (Louis Jackson); Richard Benedict ("Curly" Steffans); Buddy Lester (Vincent Massler); Sammy Davis, Jr. (Josh Howard); Angie Dickinson (Beatrice Ocean)

CREDITS: Lewis Milestone (producer and director); Harry Brown and Charles Lederer (screenplay), from a story by George Clayton Johnston and Jack Golden Russell; William H. Daniels (photography); Nelson Riddle (musical score); Nicolai Remisoff (art director); M.A. Merrick (sound); Philip W. Anderson (editor)

RUN TIME: 127 minutes

Pepe

A Posa Films and George Sidney International Pictures Production (1960)
Released by Columbia Pictures

CAST: Cantinflas (Pepe); Dan Dailey (Ted Holt); Edward G. Robinson (himself); Shirley Jones (Suzie Murphy); Carlos Montalban (Rodriguez); Vicki Trickett (Lupita); Jay North (Dennis the Menace); Ernie Kovacs (Immigration Inspector); Judy Garland (Vocalist on Radio); William Demarest (Studio Gateman); Sammy Davis, Jr. (Himself); with guest appearances including: Tony Curtis, Dean Martin, Billie Burke, Frank Sinatra, Cesar Romero, Donna Reed, Peter Lawford, Kim Novak, Maurice Chevalier, Bing Crosby, Bobby Darin, Zsa Zsa Gabor, and Janet Leigh

CREDITS: Jacques Gelman and George Sidney (producer); George Sidney (director); Claude Binyon and Dorothy Kingsley (screenplay), from story by Sonya Levien and Leonard Spigelass and a play by Leslie

Bush-Fekete; Joe MacDonald (photography); Johnny Green (musical score); Eugene Loring and Alex Romero (dance directors); Gunther Gerszo (associate art director); James Z. Flaster and Charles J. Rice (sound); Al Clark and Viola Lawrence (editors)

RUN TIME: 180 minutes

Convicts 4

A Kaufman-Lubin Production (1962)
Released by Allied Artists

CAST: Ben Gazzara (John Resko); Stuart Whitman (Principal Keeper); Ray Walston (Iggy); Vincent Price (Carl Carmer); Rod Steiger (Tiptoes); Broderick Crawford (Warden); Dodie Stevens (Resko's sister); Jack Kruschen (Resko's father); Naomi Stevens (Resko's mother); Sammy Davis, Jr. (Wino)

CREDITS: A. Ronald Lubin (producer); Millard Kaufman (director); Millard Kaufman (screenplay); Joseph Biroc (photography); Leonard Rosenman (musical score); Howard Richmond (art director); Ralph Butler (sound); George White (editor)

RUN TIME: 105 minutes

Sergeants 3

An Essex-Claude Production (1962)
Released by United Artists

CAST: Frank Sinatra (1st Sgt. Mike Merry); Dean Martin (Sgt. Chip Deal); Sammy Davis, Jr. (Jonah Williams); Peter Lawford (Sgt. Larry Barrett); Joey Bishop (Sgt. Maj. Roger Boswell); Henry Silva (Mountain Hawk); Ruta Lee (Amelia Parent); Buddy Lester (Willie Sharpknife); Phil Crosby (Corporal Ellis); Dennis Crosby (Private Page)

CREDITS: Frank Sinatra and Howard W. Koch (producers); John Sturges (director); W. R. Burnett (screenplay); Winton Hoch (photography); Billy May (musical score); Frank Hotaling (art director); Harold Lewis and Harry Alphin (sound); Ferris Webster (editor)

RUN TIME: 112 minutes

Johnny Cool

A Chrislaw Production (1963)
Released by United Artists

CAST: Henry Silva (Johnny Cool); Elizabeth Montgomery (Darien "Dare" Guiness); Richard Anderson (Correspondent); Jim Backus (Louis Murphy); Brad Dexter (Lennart Crandall); Wanda Hendrix (Miss Connolly); Hank Henry (Bus driver); Marc Lawrence (Johnny Colini); John McGiver (Oby Hinds); Sammy Davis, Jr. ("Educated")

CREDITS: William Asher and Peter Lawford (producers); William Asher (director); Joseph Landon (screenplay), from the novel *The Kingdom of Johnny Cool* by John McPartland; Sam Leavitt (photography); Billy May (musical score); Frank T. Smith (art director); Philip Mitchell (sound); Otto Ludwig (editor)

RUN TIME: 101 minutes

Three Penny Opera

A C.E.C.-Kurt Ulrich Film Production (1964)
Released by Embassy Pictures

CAST: Sammy Davis, Jr. (Ballad Singer); Kurt Jurgens (Macheath); June Ritchie (Polly Peachum); Hildegarde Knef (Pirate Jenny); Marlene Warrlich (Lucy Brown); Lino Ventura (Tiger Brown); Gert Fröbe (Peachum); Hilde Hildebrandt (Mrs. Peachum); Walter Giller (Filch)

CREDITS: Kurt Ulrich (producer); Wolfgang Staudte (director); Günter Weisenborn and Wolfgang Staudte (screenplay), from the opera *Die Dreigroschenoper* by Berthold Brecht (book and libretto) and Kurt Weill (music) which was based on the play *The Beggar's Opera* by John Gay; Roger Fellaus (photography); Peter Sandloff (musical score); Dick Price (dance director); Hein Heckroth (sets and costumes); Fritz Schwarz (sound); Wolfgang Wehrum (editor)

RUN TIME: 83 minutes

Robin and the Seven Hoods

A P-C Production (1964)
Released by Warner Bros.

CAST: Frank Sinatra (Robbo); Dean Martin (Little John); Sammy Davis, Jr. (Will); Bing Crosby (Allen A. Dale); Peter Falk (Guy Gisborne); Barbara Rush (Marian); Edward G. Robinson (Big Jim); Victor Buono (Crocker); Barry Kelley (Police Chief); Hank Henry (Six Second)

CREDITS: Frank Sinatra, Howard W. Koch, and William H. Daniels (producers); Gordon Douglas (director); David R. Schwartz (screenplay); William H. Daniels (photography); Sammy Cahn and James Van Heusen (songs); Nelson Riddle (musical score); LeRoy Deane (art director); Everett Hughes and Vinton Vernon (sound); Sam O'Steen (editor)

RUN TIME: 123 minutes

Nightmare in the Sun

An Afilmco Production (1964)
Released by Zodiac Films

CAST: Ursula Andress (Marsha); John Derek (The Hitchhiker); Aldo Ray (The Sheriff); Arthur O'Connell (Sam Wilson); Sammy Davis, Jr. (Truck driver); Allyn Joslyn (Junk dealer); Keenan Wynn (Song-and-dance misfit); Chick Chandler (Tavern owner); Richard Jaeckel (Motorcyclist); Robert Duvall (Second motorcyclist)

CREDITS: Marc Lawrence and John Derek (producers); Marc Lawrence (director); Ted Thomas and Fanya Lawrence (screenplay), from story by Marc Lawrence and George Fass; Stanley Cortez (photography); Paul Glass (musical score); Paul Sylos (art director); Glen Glenn (sound); Douglas Stewart and William Shenberg (editors)

RUN TIME: 81 minutes

A Man Called Adam

A Trace-Mark Production (1966)
Released by Embassy Pictures

CAST: Sammy Davis, Jr. (Adam Johnson); Ossie Davis (Nelson Davis); Cicely Tyson (Claudia Ferguson); Louis Armstrong (Willie "Sweet Daddy" Ferguson); Frank Sinatra Jr. (Vincent); Peter Lawford (Manny); Mel Torme (Himself); Lola Falana (Theo); Jeanette Dubois (Martha); Johnny Brown (Les)

CREDITS: Joseph E. Levine, Ike Jones, and James Waters (producers); Leo Penn (director); Les Pine and Tina Rome (screenplay); Jack Priestley (photography); Benny Carter (musical score) Charles Rosen (art director); Dennis Maitland (sound); Carl Lerner (editor)

RUN TIME: 103 minutes

Salt and Pepper

A Trace-Mark and Chrislaw Production (1968)
Released by United Artists

CAST: Sammy Davis, Jr. (Charles Salt); Peter Lawford (Christopher Pepper); Michael Bates (Inspector Crabbe); Ilona Rogers (Marianne Renaud); John Le Mesurier (Col. Woodstock); Graham Stark (Sgt. Walters); Ernest Clark (Col. Balsom); Jeanne Roland (Mai Ling); Robert Dorning (Club secretary); Robertson Hare (Dove)

CREDITS: Sammy Davis, Jr., Peter Lawford, and Milton Ebbins (producers); Richard Donner (director); Michael Pertwee (screenplay); Ken Higgins (photography); John Dankworth (musical score); Lionel Blair (dance director); Don Mingay (art director); John Poyner (sound); Jack Slade (editor)

RUN TIME: 101 minutes

Sweet Charity

A Universal Production (1969)
Released by Universal Studios

CAST: Shirley MacLaine (Charity Hope Valentine); Sammy Davis, Jr. (Big Daddy); Ricardo Montalban (Vittorio Vitale); John McMartin (Oscar Lindquist); Chita Rivera (Nickie); Paula Kelly (Helene); Stubby Kaye (Herman); Barbara Bouchet (Ursula); Alan Hewitt (Nicholsby); Dante D'Paulo (Charlie)

CREDITS: Robert Arthur (producer); Bob Fosse (director); Peter Stone (screenplay), from the play *Sweet Charity* by Neil Simon, Sy Coleman, and Dorothy Fields; Robert Surtees (photography); Joseph Gershenson (musical score); Bob Fosse (dance director); Alexander Golitzen and George C. Webb (art directors); Waldon O. Watson, William Russell, Ronald Pierce, and Len Peterson (sound); Stuart Gilmore (editor)

RUN TIME: 150 minutes

One More Time

A Trace-Mark and Chrislaw Production (1970)
Released by United Artists

CAST: Sammy Davis, Jr. (Charles Salt); Peter Lawford (Chris Pepper/Lord Sydney Pepper); Maggie Wright (Miss Tompkins); Leslie Sands (Inspector); John Wood (Figg); Sydney Arnold (Tombs); Edward Evans (Gordon); Percy Herbert (Mander); Bill Maynard (Jenson); Dudley Sutton (Wilson)

CREDITS: Sammy Davis, Jr., Peter Lawford, and Milton Ebbins (producers); Jerry Lewis (director); Michael Pertwee (screenplay); Ernest Steward (photography); Les Reed (musical score); Jack Stevens (art director); Gerry Humphreys (sound); William Butler (editor)

RUN TIME: 93 minutes

Save the Children

A Stellar Production (1973)
Released by Paramount Pictures

CAST: Performers include Sammy Davis, Jr., the Staple Singers, the Temptations, Isaac Hayes, Roberta Flack, Quincy Jones, Gladys Knight and the Pips, Nancy Wilson, the Jackson Five, and Ramsey Lewis

CREDITS: Matt Robinson and Clarence Avant (producers); Stan Lathan (director); Matt Robinson (screenplay); Cinematographers include Charles Blackwell, Bob Fletcher, Robert Grant, Doug Harris, and Rufus Hinton (photography); Gene Barge (musical score); Charles Rosen (art director); Phil Ramone (sound); George Bowers and Paul Evans (editors)

RUN TIME: 123 minutes

Sammy Stops the World

Released by Special Event Entertainment (1979)

CAST: Sammy Davis, Jr. (Littlechap); Marian Mercer (Evie/Anya/Ilse/Lorene); Marcus B.F. Brown (Ensemble member); Shelly Burch (Jane)

CREDITS: Mark Travis and Del Jack (producers); Mel Shapiro (director); based on the play *Stop the World—I Want to Get Off*, book, music, and lyrics by Leslie Bricusse and Anthony Newley (screenplay); David Myers (photography); Santo Loquasto (art director); William H. Yahraus (editor)

RUN TIME: 105 minutes

Heidi's Song

A Hanna-Barbera Production (1982)
Released by Paramount Pictures

CAST: Lorne Greene (Grandfather); Sammy Davis, Jr. (Head Ratte); Margery Gray (Heidi); Michael Bell (Willie); Peter Cullen (Gruffle); Roger DeWitt (Peter); Richard Erdman (Herr Sessman); Virginia Gregg (Aunt Dete); Janet Waldo (Tinette)

CREDITS: Joseph Barbera and William Hanna (producers); Robert Taylor (director); Jameson Brewer, Joseph Barbera, and Robert Taylor (screenplay), from the novel *Heidi* by Johanna Spyri; Hoyt S. Curtin (musical score); Paul Julian (art director); Gregory V. Watson Jr. (editor)

RUN TIME: 93 minutes

Cannonball Run II

A Warner Bros. Production (1984)
Released by Warner Communications

CAST: Burt Reynolds (J.J. McClure); Dom DeLuise (Victor/Chaos); Dean Martin (Blake); Sammy Davis, Jr. (Fenderbaum); Jamie Farr (Sheik); Marilu Henner (Betty); Telly Savalas (Hymie Kaplan); Shirley MacLaine (Veronica); Susan Anton (Jill); Catherine Bach (Marcie)

CREDITS: Albert S. Ruddy (producer); Hal Needham (director); Albert S. Ruddy, Hal Needham, and Harvey Miller (screenplay), from characters created by Brock Yates; Nick McLean (photography); Al Capps (musical score); Tho. E. Azzari (art director); William Gordean and Carl Kress (editors)

RUN TIME: 108 minutes

Tap

A Beco film and Tri-Star Production (1989)
Released by Tri-Star Pictures

CAST: Gregory Hines (Max); Suzzanne Douglas (Amy); Sammy Davis, Jr. (Little Mo); Savion Glover (Louis); Joe Morton (Nicky); Terrence E. McNally (Bob Wythe); Dick Anthony Williams (Francis); Bunny Briggs (Bunny); Steve Condos (Steve); Arthur Duncan (Arthur)

CREDITS: Gary Adelson and Richard Vane (producers); Nick Castle (director); Nick Castle (screenplay); David Gribble (photography); James Newton Howard (musical score); Patricia Norris (art director); Patrick Kennedy (editor)

RUN TIME: 111 minutes

PHOTO CREDITS

INDEX

ACKNOWLEDGMENTS

Thank you to my family:

My brothers, Mark and Jeff: love you both.

My kids, Sam, Rae (Montana), Greer, and Chase: I love you more. Pop would be so proud of all of you, as am I. Thank you so much for helping me at every turn.

Lennart Ringquist: thank you for your advice and for making Mom happy.

Guy Garner: thank you endlessly.

Mom: I love you and I thank you for retelling stories and thoughts. You helped me make this possible. Your insight is invaluable. Remember, I will always know Dad wasn't the only brave one.

Pop: all day, every day.

Billy Crystal: thank you for your many years of support and friendship to my father and my family. I know how much you loved him and treasured your time together. We love you.

Nina Bunche Pierce acknowledgments:

Thank you to Tracey Davis for fifteen years of friendship, May Britt for your candid interviews, and to Cindy De La Hoz, our editor extraordinaire.

A special thank you to videographer/editor/writer Luke Sacher and producer/director Carole Langer for sharing off-camera conversations from their documentary, *Biography: The Rat Pack*. Lastly, I would like to thank Sammy Davis Jr., who I will always think of as I do my own father—with great love, admiration, and respect.